Cultural Defences at the International Criminal Court

T0373699

Cultural defences, i.e. claims that certain aspects of a defendant's cultural background should be taken into consideration by courts when adjudicating on their guilt or innocence, have been raised before domestic courts in a variety of jurisdictions. This has been a very sensitive and controversial issue. However, the issue of cultural defences at international tribunals is one that has not yet been fully explored. The main objective of this book is to analyse if the International Criminal Court can, and should, accommodate cultural defences as answers to legal charges, or if the Court should accommodate cultural considerations in other ways.

Noelle Higgins is a Senior Lecturer in Law at Maynooth University Department of Law, Ireland.

Cultural Defences at the International Criminal Court

Noelle Higgins

Routledge
Taylor & Francis Group

LONDON AND NEW YORK

First published 2018
by Routledge

2 Park Square, Milton Park, Abingdon, Oxfordshire OX14 4RN
52 Vanderbilt Avenue, New York, NY 10017

Routledge is an imprint of the Taylor & Francis Group, an informa business

First issued in paperback 2019

British Library Cataloguing in Publication Data
A catalogue record for this book is available from the British Library

Library of Congress Cataloging in Publication Data
Names: Higgins, Noelle, author.
Title: Cultural defences at the International Criminal Court / Noelle
   Higgins.
Description: New York, NY : Routledge, 2018. | Includes bibliographical
   references and index.
Identifiers: LCCN 2017049537| ISBN 9781138893610 (hbk) | ISBN
   9781351718042 (web pdf) | ISBN 9781351718035 (epub) | ISBN
   9781351718028 (kindle)
Subjects: LCSH: Defense (International criminal procedure) | Cultural
   defense (Law) | International Criminal Court.
Classification: LCC KZ7408 .H54 2018 | DDC 345/.05044—dc23
LC record available at https://lccn.loc.gov/2017049537

ISBN: 978-1-138-89361-0 (hbk)
ISBN: 978-0-367-88897-8 (pbk)

Typeset in Times New Roman
by Swales & Willis Ltd, Exeter, Devon, UK

Contents

Acknowledgements

I would like to sincerely thank my students in Galway and in Maynooth, from whom I continue to learn! I would also like to thank my extensive support network at home and abroad, and special thanks go to Los Watkins, whose help is always appreciated.

Ba mhaith liom buíochas ó chroí a ghabháil le mo chuid mac léinn i nGaillimh agus i Maigh Nuad; bím de shíor ag foghlaim uathu! Ba mhaith liom buíochas a ghabháil freisin le mo lucht tacaíochta i bhfad agus i gcéin, agus tá buíochas speisialta ag gabháil do Los Watkins, a bhfuil meas agam ar a chuid comhairle i gcónaí.

Introduction

Introductory comments

Cultural defences, that is, claims that certain aspects of a defendant's cultural background should be taken into consideration by courts when adjudicating on their guilt or innocence, have been raised before domestic courts in a variety of jurisdictions.[1] In addition, national courts have also taken the cultural context of a defendant's actions into consideration at the sentencing phase.[2] The acceptance of cultural defences in domestic criminal law has been a very sensitive and controversial issue in various jurisdictions, encompassing different legal traditions,[3] and has both proponents and opponents in fairly equal measure. Conversely, the issue of cultural defences at international criminal tribunals is one that has not yet been fully explored. There has been little legal practice on the issue, and consequently, the vast amount of scholarship on the topic of cultural defences has, to date, been focused on the domestic realm,[4] with only a little attention being concentrated on the use of such defences at international tribunals.[5] However, an in-depth analysis of the potential use (and abuse) of the cultural defence at the International Criminal Court (ICC) is necessary and timely, given that cultural contexts of international crimes have recently been given some consideration in cases before this Court.[6]

The ICC was created in 1998, with the signing of its foundation document, the Rome Statute.[7] The Statute is the culmination of negotiations between 160 States, representing the major legal systems and cultures of the world. It is generally held that there are three major legal families in the world, i.e. common law, civil law (both Western in character) and Islamic law. When the Rome Statute came to a vote in 1998, 120 States voted in favour, while 7, including the US, China and Israel voted against and 21 abstained.

The main aim of the ICC is to deal with the worst human rights violations and the Court has jurisdiction over the crimes of genocide, war crimes, crimes against humanity and aggression. The negotiations during the Rome Conference required States from different types of legal systems to compromise on many issues, from the definition of crimes, to the limits of acceptable defences, to the rules of evidence and procedure. Each State was influenced by its own legal culture during the negotiations, with negotiators proffering ideas based on their own domestic legal system as best practice, since '[l]egal training within each domestic legal tradition determines in part lawyers' understanding of basic legal concepts. It is only natural to expect legal experts to draw upon their legal background in drafting a state's international commitments'.[8] In 1998, the percentage of civil law states in the world amounted to 51%, while common states accounted for 25%, Islamic law states made up 14%, while the remaining 10% of states had a mixed legal system.[9] Reflecting the spread of the three major legal systems, the number of Islamic law states negotiating at the Rome Conference was not as large as those representing common law and civil law traditions.[10]

The Statute entered into force on 1 July 2002, upon having been ratified by 60 States. Given the disparity in the domestic criminal legal systems represented at the Rome Conference, the fact that the Rome Statute was overwhelmingly accepted is significant. A question thus arises whether all of the legal traditions represented at the Rome Conference had an impact on the resultant Statute, i.e. does the Rome Statute adequately represent the legal systems of the world? Following on from this, are defences based on culture, which are accepted as valid in some domestic legal systems, acceptable under the Statute? This question is important, as the Statute currently has 123 ratifications,[11] and the Court can also exercise jurisdiction when the alleged perpetrator is a national of a State Party or where the crime was committed in the territory of a State Party. In addition, a State not party to the Statute may decide to accept the jurisdiction of the ICC.[12] Furthermore, the Security Council of the United Nations may refer a situation to the Court for investigation under Article 13(b) of the Rome Statute even in a State that has not ratified the Statute.[13] Therefore, the Court has a very extensive reach. If, however, the Court does not pay due regard to the legal systems and cultures of its constituent States, can justice be adequately served?

Defences are one of the most under-studied aspects of international criminal law,[14] with cultural defences in the context of international criminal law only receiving scant attention in the literature to date,[15] and indeed, much of this literature is in the field of anthropology and sociology rather than law.[16] While the Rome Statute does not explicitly allow for a cultural defence to be raised, neither does it prohibit it. Article 31 of the Statute sets out circumstances that can exclude the criminal responsibility of defendants. These are: mental incapacity, intoxication, self-defence and duress. Article 32 also allows for the defence of mistake of law or fact and Article 33 allows for the defence of superior orders. These provisions are not elaborated on in detail, and, therefore, it is necessary to analyse whether cultural considerations could be encompassed within any of these explicit defences. Article 31 also states that the list of defences is not exhaustive, and therefore, it is also necessary to investigate whether cultural considerations could be included in any other international criminal law defences, and thus be raised before the ICC.

Research question

This book deals with the role of cultural defences at the ICC, and focuses on two main issues: first, it analyses whether if, in theory, cultural defences can be brought before the ICC. Second, it queries whether cultural defences should be accepted by the Court in practice.

The need to examine cultural defences at the ICC is pressing for a number of reasons. First, the importance of culture in a person's life is undeniable. Stamatopoulou comments that '[c]ulture is inseparable from the quality of being human, from the sense of self-respect of a person or a community'.[17] In a similar vein, Dundes Renteln and Valladares state that

> [i]t is difficult to overstate the importance of culture and the subtle pressure it exerts on individuals. Culture is pervasive and all-encompassing; it shapes perceptions and affects behavior in every society, even though individuals are largely unaware of these processes.[18]

Therefore, while a person's culture may not determine a defendant's motivations and / or actions, they can be heavily influenced by it.[19]

In addition, there are also human rights arguments in favour of allowing defendants to present cultural evidence in the courtroom,[20] including the right to culture,[21] and the right to a fair trial.[22] Given that the Rome Statute provides that the ICC can consider 'internationally recognized human rights' in its interpretation of applicable law,[23] it seems incumbent on the Court to analyse the consequences of these rights in the context of cultural defences.

Furthermore, if the ICC were to allow a defence based on culture, this may serve to improve the Court's reputation against claims of the anti-African bias, which have plagued the institution in recent times.[24] Given that Western States had significantly more impact on the drafting of the Rome Statute than non-Western States, if it were seen that the cultures of non-Western States were given due consideration in the deliberations and decisions of the Court, this may (re)legitimise the Court in some quarters.

However, the acceptance of cultural defences at the ICC would bring with it a number of problems, including challenges to the principle of equality as individuals may not be treated the same if they come from different cultural backgrounds,[25] and challenges to deciphering the limits of 'culture'. The acceptance of cultural defences would also entail a number of practical difficulties, including evaluating expert testimony in the Court.[26]

Structure

In order to adequately address the research question, Chapter 1 first analyses how cultural defences have been used in domestic criminal law and weighs up the disadvantages and advantages of allowing such defences a place in the legal system. Chapter 2 then focuses on the ICC and discusses the legal traditions that impacted on the drafting of the Rome Statute. This Chapter analyses the cultural diversity of the Court and queries whether the major legal systems of the world are well served by the Court through cultural accommodation measures in the legal framework. As part of this discussion, a study will be made of the sources of law, on which the Court can depend, as set out in Article 21 of the Statute, particularly 'general principles of law'. Chapter 3 undertakes an examination of the legal framework in the Rome Statute concerning defences and it investigates whether cultural defences can be encompassed in the explicit defences set out in the Statute or in other international criminal law defences. The early practice of the Court with regard to cultural considerations is considered in Chapter 4. While the Court has not accepted a cultural defence (as yet), cultural issues were raised in the case of *Prosecutor v Al Mahdi*[27] and the Court is currently dealing with a different set of cultural concerns in the case of *Prosecutor v Ongwen*.[28] The book finishes with a number of conclusions as to whether the Rome Statute can, in theory, accommodate cultural defences, and a number of recommendations as to whether it should do so in practice.

Notes

1 See Julia P Sams, 'The Availability of the "Cultural Defense" as an Excuse for Criminal Behavior' (1986) 16 *Georgia Journal of International and Comparative Law* 335; Jeroen Van Broeck, 'Cultural Defence and Culturally Motivated Crimes (Cultural Offences) (2001) 9(1) *European Journal of Crime, Criminal Law and Criminal Justice* 1; M-C Foblets, 'Cultural Delicts: The Repercussion of Cultural Conflicts on Delinquent Behaviour. Reflections on the Contribution of Legal Anthropology to a Contemporary Debate' (1998) 6 *European Journal of Crime, Criminal Law and Criminal Justice* 187; and Carolyn Choi, 'Application of a Cultural Defense in Criminal Proceedings' (1990) 8(1) *Pacific Basin Law Journal* 80.
2 See Van Broeck (n1).
3 See Van Broeck (n1).

4 See Alison Dundes Renteln, 'Making Room for Culture in the Court' (2010) 49 *The Judges Journal* 7; Alison Dundes Renteln and Rene Valladares, 'The Importance of Culture for the Justice System' (2009) 92 *Judicature* 193; and Alison Dundes Renteln, 'The Use and Abuse of the Cultural Defence' in Marie-Claire Foblets and Alison Dundes Renteln (eds), *Multicultural Jurisprudence* (Hart Publishing 2009), 61.

5 See Alison Dundes Renteln, 'Cultural Defenses in International Criminal Trials: A Preliminary Consideration of the Issues' (2011) 18 *Southwestern Journal of International Law* 267; Mike Farrell *et al.*, 'War Crimes and other Human Rights Abuses in the Former Yugoslavia' (1995) 16 *Whittier Law Review* 374; Alison Dundes Renteln, 'The Child Soldier: The Challenge of Enforcing International Standards' (1999) 21 *Whittier Law Review* 191; Ida L Bostian, 'Cultural Relativism in International War Crimes Prosecutions: The International Criminal Tribunal for Rwanda' (2005) 12 *International Law Students Association Journal of International and Comparative Law* 1.

6 See, for example, *Prosecutor v Al Mahdi*, ICC-01/12-01/15 and *Prosecutor v Ongwen*, ICC-02/04-01/15.

7 Rome Statute of the International Criminal Court 1998, UN Doc A/CONF.183/9. Hereinafter, Rome Statute.

8 Emilia Justyna Powell and Sara Mitchell, 'The Creation and Expansion of the International Criminal Court: A Legal Explanation' (Midwest Political Science Association Conference, Chicago, Illinois, 3–6 April 2008) http://ir.uiowa.edu/polisci_pubs/3/ accessed 2 October 2017.

9 *Ibid.*

10 *Ibid.*

11 See: https://asp.icc-cpi.int/en_menus/asp/states%20parties/pages/the%20states%20parties%20to%20the%20rome%20statute.aspx accessed 2 October 2017.

12 The Ivory Coast recognised the jurisdiction of the ICC in April 2003, and subsequently ratified the Statute on 15 February 2013. See: www.icc-cpi.int/pages/situations.aspx accessed 2 October 2017.

13 The Security Council referred the situations of Sudan (March 2005) and Libya (February 2011) to the Court and investigations were subsequently opened. See: www.icc-cpi.int/pages/situations.aspx accessed 2 October 2017.

14 See Robert Cryer *et al.*, *An Introduction to International Criminal Law and Procedure* (3rd edn, Cambridge University Press 2014), 398. The seminal work on defences in international criminal law is Geert-Jan Alexander Knoops, *Defences in Contemporary International Criminal Law* (2nd edn Martinus Nijhoff 2008).

15 See however, Tim Kelsall, *Culture under Cross-examination: International Justice and the Special Court for Sierra Leone* (Cambridge University Press 2009).

16 See Richard Ashby Wilson, 'Expert Evidence on Trial: Social Researchers in the International Criminal Courtroom' (2016) 43(4) *American Ethnologist* 730. See also Nigel Eltringham, '"Illuminating the Broader Context": Anthropological and Historical Knowledge at the International Criminal Tribunal for Rwanda' (2013) 19 *Journal of the Royal Anthropological Institute* 338.

17 Elsa Stamatopoulou, *The Right to Culture in International Law* (Brill 2007), 107–108.

18 Alison Dundes Renteln and Rene Valladares (n 4), 194.

19 *Ibid.*, 194.

20 *Ibid.*, 196.

21 See Article 27(1), Universal Declaration of Human Rights, 1948, proclaimed by the United Nations General Assembly in Paris on 10 December 1948 General Assembly resolution 217(III), which states: 'Everyone has the right freely to participate in the cultural life of the community, to enjoy the arts and to share in scientific advancement and its benefits.' The right to culture is developed in subsequent international instruments, including the International Covenant on Economic, Social and Cultural Rights, Adopted and opened for signature, ratification and accession by General Assembly resolution 2200A (XXI) of 16 December 1966. The right to culture is also promoted and protected in regional human rights instruments, including Article 17 of the African Charter on Human and Peoples' Rights, adopted 27 June 1981, OAU Doc. CAB/LEG/67/3 rev. 5, 21 I.L.M. 58 (1982), entered into force 21 October 1986; Article 26 of the American Convention on Human Rights, adopted at the Inter-American Specialized Conference on Human Rights, San José, Costa Rica, 22 November 1969, and Article 42 of the Arab Charter on Human Rights, adopted by the League of Arab States, 22 May 2004, entered into force 15 March 2008.

22 See Alison Dundes Renteln (2011) (n 5), 267. The right to a fair trial is protected in Article 14 of the International Covenant on Civil and Political Rights and Article 14 of the International Covenant on Economic, Social and Cultural Rights, GA Res 2200 (XXI) A, UN GAOR, 21st Sess. Supp. No 16, UN Doc A/6316, at 49. At a regional level, this right is protected in Article 6 of the European Convention for the Protection of Human Rights and Fundamental Freedoms 1953 UNTS 222, Articles 5, 6 and 7 of the Charter of Fundamental Rights of the European Union, 2000 OJ (C 364) 1, 9, Articles 3, 7 and 26 of the African Charter on Human and People's Rights 1981, OAU Doc CAB/LEG/67/3 rev 5, 21 ILM 58, Articles 3, 8, 9 and 10 of the American Convention on Human Rights, 1969, OAST No 36 1144 UNTS 123.

23 Article 21(3) of the Rome Statute. See Rebecca Young, '"Internationally Recognized Human Rights" before the International Criminal Court' (2011) 60(1) *International and Comparative Law Quarterly* 189.

24 The anti-African bias has led to a situation whereby members of the African Union have backed a Kenyan proposal to leave the ICC. See Fatou Bensouda, 'The International Criminal Court and Africa: A Discussion on Legitimacy, Impunity, Selectivity, Fairness and Accountability, (Keynote address, GIMPA Law Conference 2016, Accra, Ghana, 17 March 2016) www.icc-cpi.int/iccdocs/ otp/Keynote_Speech_of_the_ProsecutorGIMPA_Law_Conference_on_ the_ICC_and_Africa.pdf accessed 2 October 2017. See also Max du Plessis, Tiyanjana Maluwa and Annie O'Reilly, *Africa and the International Criminal Court* (Chatham House Report, International Law 2013/01 2013); Konstantinos D Magliveras and Gino J Naldi, 'The International Criminal Courts Involvement with Africa: Evaluation of a Fractious Relationship' (2013) 82(3) *Nordic Journal of International Law* 417. However, the ICC has recently focused its attention on places other than Africa, including Palestine and Georgia.

25 James M Donovan and John Stuart Garth, 'Delimiting the Cultural Defense' (2007) 26 *Quinnipiac Law Review* 109, 110.

26 See Richard Ashby Wilson (n 16).

27 *Prosecutor v Al Mahdi* (n 6).

28 *Prosecutor v Ongwen* (n 6).

1 The cultural defence: its use and abuse

Introduction

The cultural context of defendants' actions has been considered in criminal cases in a variety of jurisdictions,[1] in legislation,[2] in plea negotiations,[3] as a defence to a charge,[4] and, most notably, as mitigation in sentencing.[5] While no State explicitly incorporates a specific cultural defence into their criminal law, defence lawyers have been willing to raise the cultural context of the clients' actions throughout different stages of the criminal process. This occurs most often in States that have a culturally diverse population, such as the United Kingdom (UK), the United States (US) and Australia, because, logically, in such States 'opportunities for cultural misunderstandings are greater, and legal systems must be prepared to consider cultural arguments'.[6] Cultural arguments are made because it is believed that culture shapes a person's understandings and influences their behaviour to a significant extent.[7] While defence lawyers are frequently willing to raise cultural issues on behalf of their clients, these are often dismissed out of hand by a court as there is no official 'cultural defence', e.g. in the US case of *State v Bauer*,[8] when the district court precluded any evidence and testimony about the defendants' religion as a legal defence to the use or possession of marijuana, despite the fact that they were Rastafarians and used marijuana in religious ceremonies.[9]

Some commentators suggest that if judicial systems allow for cultural considerations, then the cultural defence should be seen as a separate, self-contained defence, while others view it as fitting into pre-existing defences.[10] For example, in the case of *People v Kimura*,[11] in the US, the defence included various cultural arguments during the plea negotiation stage. Ms Kimura, who was born in Japan and raised there until she was 19, found that her husband was having an affair. She became overwhelmed with shame that she had not been a good enough wife and decided to engage in the ancient Japanese ritual of *oyako shinju*, i.e. parent–child suicide, by drowning in the ocean. Her children drowned but she was rescued, and subsequently charged with first degree murder. The defence illustrated, with the help of mental health experts, that Ms Kimura had been suffering from insanity at the time of the drowning, which emanated from culturally induced feelings of disgrace. Despite the fact that *oyako shinju* was illegal in Japan at the time, the practice still continued, and the Japanese–American community organised a petition asking that the District Attorney's Office show leniency as, it was argued, the defendant's actions 'were based on a different worldview'.[12] The case was settled through plea negotiations, with the charge being reduced to voluntary manslaughter, and Ms Kimura was sentenced to one year in jail and five years' probation with conditions.

In most cases, cultural factors only play a part at the sentencing stage of a case as a mitigating factor, such as in the case of *R v Ipeelee* before the Canadian Supreme Court, where the Court highlighted that in sentencing Aboriginal offenders judges have to take judicial notice of

> the history of colonialism, displacement, and residential schools and how that history continues to translate into lower educational attainment, lower incomes, higher unemployment, higher rates of substance abuse and suicide, and of course higher levels of incarceration for Aboriginal peoples.[13]

It is clear, therefore, that domestic practice on cultural defences is diverse and *ad hoc*. In addition, judicial and academic commentary on the cultural defence has varied hugely, with both proponents and opponents arguing about its potential use and abuse.[14] The case for allowing a cultural defence is controversial because this would allow for people to be treated differently in a court of law, based on their cultural background, flying in the face of the principle of equality before the law. There are numerous other vociferous objections to the cultural defence, including cultural relativism, and the abuse of the concept of 'culture'. On the other hand, however, there are significant multilayered arguments proffered in support of accepting defences based on culture, including tenets of international human rights law, and the theory of individualised justice. [15]

While much uncertainty surrounds the defence, and many arguments exist as to why or why not it should be accepted, the fact remains that the cultural defence has succeeded in a number of criminal cases in a variety of jurisdictions. Should a similar defence, therefore, also be allowed to be raised in international trials in general, and before the ICC in particular? In order to answer this query, a review of current practice and opinion concerning the cultural defence is required and this is the purpose of this present Chapter. The next section of this Chapter focuses on defining culture and explaining the term cultural defence. The final section then assesses the arguments in favour and against the acceptance of cultural defences that have been put forward in the literature.

What is 'culture'?

It has been stated that '[a]s a general question of social science, the meaning of culture is difficult and controversial'[16] and it is a concept that is 'notoriously resistant to definition'.[17] This is because the concept of culture is a contested one, meaning different things to different people, and can change over time.[18] Therefore, its contours have not been definitely identified. The UN Committee on Economic, Social and Cultural Rights in General Comment 21 states that '[i]n the Committee's view, culture is a broad, inclusive concept encompassing all manifestations of human existence'[19], highlighting the vastness of the concept, leading Kymlicka *et al.* to comment that

> [i]n our view, there is little to be gained by trying to come up with a definition of 'culture.' This has proven to be a hopeless task in many disciplines. Even sophisticated attempts to define the concept of culture quickly prove unwieldy.[20]

This is understandable given the multifarious aspects of culture and the vast differences between cultures the world over. However, the lack of a universally accepted definition of culture weakens the argument to accept cultural defences.

The cultural defence[21]

The term 'cultural defence' has been defined to include 'all possible settings in which cultural factors affect the penal liability of individuals in cases brought before the court'.[22] However, the term is also sometimes extended to include cultural features that are presented throughout the course of a case, including plea bargaining or mitigating factors with respect to a defendant's sentence, thus encompassing both liability and mitigation issues. At the level of the ICC, the cultural context of a defendant's behaviour at the reparations stage of the case can also be considered.

Cultural defences are part of the cultural accommodation process in the criminal justice system,[23] which is manifested in many forms, from enacting legislation in respect of criminalising attacks on minority groups, to exempting certain groups from some laws on religious grounds, to guaranteeing access to an interpreter, to ensuring that judicial appointments and jury selection reflect the cultural makeup of the State.[24] The cultural defence element of cultural accommodation focuses on arguments made on behalf of the defendant and based on his / her culture. The term 'cultural defences' in this work, therefore, is not limited to a 'defence' in the strict sense but encompasses cultural considerations that are raised by a defendant at all stages of his / her trial.

Arguments in favour of and against the cultural defence

The right to culture

One of the main arguments put forward by proponents of the cultural defence is that international human rights law places an obligation on States to respect the culture of people within their jurisdiction. Despite a lack of definition of 'culture', the right to culture has been enshrined in a number of international human rights instruments. However, the challenge of defining 'culture' is significant, and this has led to a lack of engagement with this subject both by academics and by international bodies, including the United Nations. In addition, other factors have meant that cultural rights have been neglected, including the fact that governments tend to fear the promotion of the creation of group identities in case such groups pose a threat to territorial integrity. Stamatopoulou also suggests that cultural rights may be regarded by some as a luxury, and, therefore, only applicable in societies that have already attained a certain level of development.[25] However, she continues,

> [n]obody could deny, by looking at human history throughout the centuries, that economic development generally goes with cultural development; culture represents the soul, the moral edifice, the self-definition and self-esteem of a person or a community, without which life loses context and meaning. In that sense, cultural development is not a luxury but a tool for obtaining 'bread and water'.[26]

Creating a legal framework

The drafting committee of the Universal Declaration of Human Rights (UDHR) was faced with numerous difficulties when drafting a provision concerning the right to culture.[27] The resultant provision, Article 27,[28] does not provide any guidance on the definition of culture or its limits but does recognise that a right to participate in cultural life exists. It seems to presuppose that there is only one culture within a State as it provides that 'everyone has the right freely to participate in the cultural life of the community', and is thus, very narrow in scope. Further efforts to provide a legal framework to the concept of culture are found in other provisions in binding international human rights treaties, the main provision being Article 15 of the International Covenant on Economic, Social and Cultural Rights (ICESCR), which states:

1 The States Parties to the present Covenant recognize the right of everyone:

   (a) To take part in cultural life;
   (b) To enjoy the benefits of scientific progress and its applications;
   (c) To benefit from the protection of the moral and material interests resulting from any scientific, literary or artistic production of which he is the author.

2 The steps to be taken by the States Parties to the present Covenant to achieve the full realization of this right shall include those necessary for the conservation, the development and the diffusion of science and culture.

3 The States Parties to the present Covenant undertake to respect the freedom indispensable for scientific research and creative activity.

4 The States Parties to the present Covenant recognize the benefits to be derived from the encouragement and development of international contacts and co-operation in the scientific and cultural fields.

Again, the right to take part in cultural life is reiterated but no real definition or elucidation on the nature of this right is forthcoming from this provision. Article 27 of the International Covenant on Civil and Political Rights (ICCPR) also deals with cultural rights, specifically the cultural rights of people belonging to minority groups. Thus, this provision is significant in multicultural States where various different cultures are present. This provision states:

In those States in which ethnic, religious or linguistic minorities exist, persons belonging to such minorities shall not be denied the right, in community with the other members of their group, to enjoy their own culture, to profess and practise their own religion, or to use their own language.[29]

While the linkage between minority groups and the right to culture is an important development in this provision, the contours of the right are still left undefined.

The right to culture is reflected in a variety of ways in other core United Nations human rights treaties, including Article 5 of Convention on the Elimination of All Forms of Discrimination against Women (CEDAW),[30] Article 8, Article 17, Article 20, Article 23, Article 24(3), Article 29(1)(c), Article 30, Article 31 of the Convention on the Rights of the Child (CRC),[31] and Article 31 on the UN Convention on Migrant Workers.[32] In addition, the right to culture is also enshrined in other UN instruments, including Article 1 and Article 4 of the Declaration on the Rights of Declaration on the Rights of Persons belonging to National or Ethnic, Religious and Linguistic Minorities.[33] Various other UN instruments require States to protect and promote cultural rights, including UNESCO documents[34] and ILO Conventions pertaining to indigenous peoples.[35] Furthermore, at the regional level, cultural rights are also protected in a number of human rights instruments, including the African Charter on Human and Peoples' Rights,[36] and the European Framework Convention for the Protection of National Minorities.[37] The Additional Protocol to the American Convention on Human Rights in the Area of Economic, Social and Cultural Rights echoes the UDHR in respect of cultural rights, and Article 22 of the Charter of Fundamental Rights of the European Union also provides that the Union 'shall respect cultural, religious and linguistic diversity'.[38]

It is clear, therefore, that the right to culture has been firmly established in international law. The scope of the right and, concomitantly, the extent to which this right places obligations on States, and indeed, to what extent domestic courts must facilitate this right by allowing cultural defences to be raised, is, however, unclear. Under Article 2 of ICESCR, States Parties undertake

> to take steps, individually and through international assistance and co-operation, especially economic and technical, to the maximum of its available resources, with a view to achieving progressively the full realization of the rights recognized in the present Covenant by all appropriate means, including particularly the adoption of legislative measures

and to guarantee these rights without discrimination. The provision also states that developing countries 'may determine to what extent they would guarantee the economic rights recognized in the present Covenant to non-nationals'. General Comment 21 of the Economic, Social and Cultural Rights Committee interprets Article 15 of ICESCR and states that this provision

> includes the right of minorities and of persons belonging to minorities to take part in the cultural life of society, and also to conserve, promote and develop their own culture. This right entails the obligation of States parties to recognize, respect and protect minority cultures as an essential component of the identity of the States themselves. Consequently, minorities have the right to their cultural diversity, traditions, customs, religion, forms of education, languages, communication media (press, radio, television, Internet) and other manifestations of their cultural identity and membership.[39]

The General Comment also focuses on cultural diversity and states: 'The protection of cultural diversity is an ethical imperative, inseparable from respect for human dignity. It implies a commitment to human rights and fundamental freedoms and requires the full implementation of cultural rights. . .'[40]

Significantly, the General Comment also deals with the legal obligations incumbent on States parties of ICESCR. This states that there is an obligation to respect, protect and fulfil the obligations of the Covenant. The Committee states that

> the obligation to respect requires States parties to refrain from interfering, directly or indirectly, with the enjoyment of the right to take part in cultural life. The obligation to protect requires States parties to take steps to prevent third parties from interfering in the right to take part in cultural life. Lastly, the obligation to fulfil requires States parties to take appropriate legislative, administrative, judicial, budgetary, promotional and other measures aimed at the full realization of the right enshrined in article 15, paragraph 1 (a), of the Covenant.[41]

In addition, the General Comment states that

> [v]iolations of article 15, paragraph 1 (a), also occur through the omission or failure of a State party to take the necessary measures to comply with its legal obligations under this provision. Violations through omission include the failure to take appropriate steps to achieve the full realization of the right of everyone to take part in cultural life, and the failure to enforce relevant laws or to provide administrative, judicial or other appropriate remedies to enable people to exercise in full the right to take part in cultural life.[42]

Can a right to raise a cultural defence be interpreted from the General Comment? A broad and very generous interpretation of the view of the Committee may conclude that a defendant's cultural context must be allowed to be raised in courts in States parties to the ICESCR, given the Committee's comments in respect of 'judicial measures' and 'judicial remedies', although this argument would not be without its critics, as being a bridge too far. A similar argument could be made in respect of Article 27 of the ICCPR, with regard to the rights of minority groups.[43] Dundes Renteln comments that

> [i]t is my view that the right to culture should, at the very least, be construed to allow individuals to present information concerning their cultural background in a court of law. The international community considers the right to culture a powerful norm that clearly imposes duties on states.[44]

She continues, stating,

> [i]nsofar as states take seriously their obligation to fulfill the right to culture required by Article 27 of the ICCPR, there is a compelling argument for the judicial consideration of cultural evidence necessary for the foundation of cultural defense claims in the courtroom.[45]

It is important to note, however, that while States parties to the ICESCR and the ICCPR are bound by these instruments, and therefore, may be required to admit evidence of cultural practices and customs in their courts, neither instrument is universally ratified,[46] meaning that such an requirement is not universal.[47]

Cultural relativism

One of the main issues at the core of the difficulty in defining culture and legislating for the right to culture, and also accepting a cultural defence in domestic law, is cultural relativism.[48] This view holds that all beliefs, customs, and practices should be understood as being specific to an individual within his / her own social context and culture, rather than being judged against the culture of another. What is regarded as a manifestation of culture to some may be an abhorrent practice to others; what is considered moral and 'right' in one society may be considered immoral and 'wrong' in another, and, because a universal standard of morality does not exist, it is impossible to judge another society's customs. Stamatopolou comments that

> [t]he prevalent attitude among many human rights experts, including international law specialists, is to avoid discussion of cultural rights lest the lurking issue of cultural relativism appears, implicitly or explicitly, to undermine the delicate and fragile universality concept that has been painstakingly woven over the last five decades.[49]

Numerous human rights instruments adopted since the UDHR have addressed the clash between respect for cultural diversity and the importance of basic human rights protections, including Article 7 of the Convention on the Elimination of All Forms of Racial Discrimination (CERD),[50] Article 5 of CEDAW,[51] Article 24 of CRC,[52] Articles 4 and 8 of the Declaration on the Rights of Persons Belonging to National or Ethnic, Religious and Linguistic Minorities[53] and Article 2 of the Declaration on the Elimination of Violence against Women.[54]

Furthermore, UN human rights treaty monitoring bodies have consistently underlined governments' obligations to abolish practices that violate human rights, even when framed as a cultural practice,[55] and have again and again highlighted the primacy of human rights law. These bodies have stated that a number of cultural practices violate human rights law, including female genital mutilation, polygamy and honour killings.[56] Furthermore, Article 4 of the UNESCO Universal Declaration on Cultural Diversity 2001 states that no one may invoke cultural diversity to infringe upon human rights guaranteed by international laws, nor to limit their scope.[57]

Enculturation

As part of the issue of cultural defences the question of if, and / or, to what extent, culture actually impacts on a person's motivations and actions arises. In this context the concept of enculturation needs to be explored. Enculturation is 'the process by which an individual learns the traditional content of a culture and assimilates its practices and values'.[58] These assimilated practices and values exert a significant, and sometimes, subconscious influence on people, and '[t]hose who presume that individuals can easily modify their behavior do not appreciate the force of enculturation'.[59] On this point, Parekh comments that

> [d]iscussion of cultural defense sometimes goes wrong because it fails to understand the nature of culture and the individual's relation to it . . . As thinking beings, human beings act on the basis of how they understand themselves and their situation, and that in turn is shaped by their culture. They do, of course, reflect on their culture, criticize and revise it, add to it elements derived from others, even replace it with another, but they cannot transcend or operate outside the realm of culture altogether. In this basic sense human beings are cultural beings.[60]

The raising of cultural evidence therefore, it is argued, provides a context for the defendant's actions and his / her motivations for these actions, which can aid the court in establishing liability or ruling on a suitable sentence.[61]

However, while culture can exert a significant influence over a person, this is not to say that a person's behaviour is completely determined by their culture, but rather a person may be predisposed to act in a particular way as a result of their cultural background. Humans retain agency over the actions,[62] and thus the cultural defence is not, by any means, an unlimited defence. In this context, it is noted that culture evolves over time and is not monolithic.[63] In addition, a defendant may also be exposed to other cultures apart from their native culture, which may open up 'an awareness of alternatives' which would give a defendant options with regard to their thinking and behaviour.[64]

Religion as culture

Some practices that are regarded as cultural may have religion at their core, as will be seen in the case of *Prosecutor v Al Mahdi* before the ICC in Chapter 4. As Stamatopolou comments, '[r]eligion is closely linked to culture and therefore respect for freedom of religion is an important element for the right to participate in culture, not only of religious minorities but also of national or ethnic minorities and indigenous peoples'.[65] Therefore, the right to freedom of religion under international human rights law must also be considered when assessing the case for accepting cultural defences. Article 18 of the ICCPR guarantees the right to religious liberty.[66] As with the cultural rights examined above, this right is general in nature, stating that

> [e]veryone shall have the right to freedom of thought, conscience and religion. This right shall include freedom to have or to adopt a religion or belief of his choice, and freedom, either individually or in community with others and in public or private, to manifest his religion or belief in worship, observance, practice and teaching.

Given that everyone is free to practise their religion or belief, this can include some religious practices that may have a cultural aspect. This provision, it is argued, gives additional support to the cultural rights espoused in the ICCPR and the ICESCR in the context of cultural defences. In this vein, Dundes Renteln comments that '[t]he right to religious liberty, protected in both domestic and international law, should also authorize defendants to explain their religious customs to courts'.[67]

The right to a fair trial

The right to a fair trial lies at the heart of all criminal trials in democratic States. This right has been enshrined in numerous domestic and international human rights law provisions,[68] and indeed, it is a central tenet of the Rome Statute of the ICC.[69] A number of arguments, both in favour of, and against, the acceptance of cultural defences emanate from this right. The argument that cultural defences should be accepted to ensure the right to a fair trial may have more traction than the right to culture argument as it is a more widely known, and accepted, right, and has a firm place in the domestic law of democratic States.[70] However, 'fairness' is quite a nebulous concept, and no provisions concerning the right to fair trial explicitly include the right of a defendant to introduce cultural evidence in support of his case.

Article 14 of the ICCPR states that '[a]ll persons shall be equal before the courts and tribunals'. Echoing this, Article 67 of the Rome Statute states that defendants are entitled to a number of minimum guarantees, 'in full equality'.[71] Thus, according to both provisions, the principle of equality is an aspect of the right to a fair trial. Opponents of the cultural defence argue that if we are to accept that a person's specific culture or religion is responsible for their actions, then we would not be treating everyone equally or judging everyone by the same yardstick.[72] This, it is argued, could lead to anarchy, and fly in the face of the principle of equality before the law.[73] On the other hand, proponents of the cultural defence refer to the Aristotelian conception of equality, which holds that unequals should be treated unequally in order to attain true equality.[74] In this vein, Truffin and Arjona comment that

> [t]raditionally, contemporary progressive thinking in the West has con-
> ceptualised the practice of equality in absolute terms; that is, treating
> everybody alike. However, the practical significance of a more sophis-
> ticated concept of equality, as defined by the Aristotelian formula of
> justice (treating like cases alike and different case differently), becomes
> evident when dealing with situations of cultural pluralism.[75]

At the domestic level, this argument would be particularly pertinent in a multicultural society with various minority groups, but whose legal system has been influenced by the majority.

Human rights treaties and the ICC

It is clear from the above discussion that a number of arguments in favour of accepting cultural defences at the domestic level focus on international human rights law. Transplanting cultural defences to the international crim-inal law level raises questions as to what extent international human rights provisions on the rights to culture, and the right to religion, impact on the ICC, as human rights treaties bind States and not courts. As stated above, the ICC Statute sets out the right to a fair trial and echoes Article 14 of the ICCPR. However, neither the right to culture, nor the right to freedom of religion are included in the instrument. The cultural diversity of the Court and the various influences on its development will be analysed in Chapter 2, however, for now, it is pertinent to note that the Preamble of the Rome Statute states that 'all peoples are united by common bonds, their cultures pieced together in a shared heritage'.[76] In addition, and as will be discussed in more depth in Chapter 2, Article 21(1)(b) includes 'applicable treaties and the principles and rules of international law', as a source of law which the ICC can apply. This, of course, would include treaties that include the right to culture and freedom of religion. Van den Herik comments that

> [t]he last two decades witnessed the spectacular promotion of international criminal law as a new sub-discipline of international law. The human rights movement constituted one of the strongest forces in this rise. For instance, as is well-known, it was a vigorous advocate in the campaign for a permanent International Criminal Court. In this dynamic, the ICC was perceived as an additional enforcement mechanism to address the most severe human rights violations.[77]

It follows, therefore, that international criminal law must take human rights seriously, including the right to culture. However, the right to culture, as a second generation right, has not received the attention it deserves within the application of international criminal law. Van den Herik continues, stating that

> [e]conomic, social and cultural rights have, so far, less directly inspired the development of international criminal law, if at all. The bias against socio-economic and cultural rights might be explained by the traditional conceptualization of this generation of human rights as having the character of programmatic aspirations rather than justiciable rights.[78]

Given the lack of engagement between international criminal law with economic, social and cultural rights, the impact of international human rights provisions on the ICC may be minimal. This, in turn, may weaken the argument for the acceptance of cultural defences at the Court.

Individualised justice

One of the main arguments in favour of accepting cultural evidence in criminal cases is that it contextualises the defendant's actions. In taking defendants' culture into consideration, the court attempts to genuinely understand them and their behaviour and to take account of their motivations for the behaviour. If defendants are not allowed to present evidence that explains the motivation for their actions, the court will be unable to reach a just verdict. In situations where a person's behaviour is based on a little known minority custom, it is argued that the court must allow for cultural evidence to be presented in order to reveal the whole story.[79] In such situations, the need to allow expert witnesses who can adequately explain cultural customs is clear. In some cases, this may be an anthropologist and in others it may be a respected elder of a minority group, and in some cases, both may be necessary to provide a complete analysis of the custom.[80]

Allowing cultural evidence to be presented can make a court's decision / punishment more acceptable to the defendant and also legitimatise the justice system.[81] Unless a court can contextualise the defendant's actions, it risks doing them an injustice, and imposing a slanted view of justice. Therefore, '[a] good case for cultural defense can be made on the ground that it improves the quality, indeed, is the very precondition of justice'.[82] This approach follows the individualised justice doctrine,[83] which focuses on providing an individualised justice process, which is tailored 'to the particular offence, the particular offender and the particular facts of the case'.[84] Parekh comments that '[a]ll justice is individualized justice in the sense that it relates to *this* defendant not anyone else, and to *this* action and not one that abstractly or superficially looks like it but is really quite different'.[85] However, in the context of cultural defences, a court must not just look at this defendant, but also at this defendant's culture and how it has impacted on his actions.[86]

An individualised justice approach has been used in sentencing in cases in a number of jurisdictions, including those with an indigenous population.[87] In these cases, a defendant's culture is treated in the same way as other factors that may influence a person's behaviour, including age, gender, socio-economic level etc., leading Dundes Renteln to comment that '[i]nsofar as individualized justice is an accepted part of legal systems, the cultural difference is simply another factor to review in the context of meting out condign punishments'.[88]

Conclusion

Defendants have raised arguments based on their cultural background in cases in a variety of jurisdictions, with varying degrees of success. Such arguments have taken different forms, some as a standalone defence, some as an aspect of an established defence such as insanity, and have been raised at different stages of the criminal process. Reviewing practice from a number of jurisdictions, it seems unlikely that States will incorporate an official cultural defence into their legal systems.[89] However, at the same time, it seems likely that arguments will continue to be made on cultural grounds on the behalf of defendants, particularly in culturally diverse jurisdictions. Dundes Renteln states that the main benefit of a State adopting an official cultural defence would be that it

> would ensure the consideration of cultural evidence in a court of law. Rather than leaving the decision about the appropriateness of admitting evidence to the whims of particular judges, a formal policy would guarantee that the courtroom door is open to data of this kind.[90]

Similarly, Parekh comments that

> [w]hile some forms of cultural defense can be subsumed under existing categories, others cannot and need to be considered on their own terms. Furthermore there are good reasons to acknowledge cultural defense in its own right. It leads to greater clarity and openness about the nature of the defense, and both the defendant and the prosecution know what sorts of arguments are expected of them. . . .It also has the additional advantage of not stretching the existing legal categories to render them vacuous or indeterminate.[91]

Despite the potential benefits of adopting an official cultural defence, this move does not seem very realistic any time soon, given the paucity of consistent practice in any jurisdiction, the weakness of international law concerning cultural rights, and the fear that such a defence may contravene key legal principles of equality before the law and non-discrimination. Amirthalingam takes a different, perhaps more conservative, approach, stating that '[i]t may be more productive to simply reform and enhance the scope of existing defences by adopting a more culturally inclusive approach to criminal law'.[92] He thus argues that a more culturally sensitive interpretation and application of established defences is a preferable approach.[93] However, while this approach may not be as controversial as adopting a distinct cultural defence, the practicalities of how to ensure that such a culturally sensitive interpretation would occur are unclear. Nevertheless, it seems that, for the moment, defence lawyers will continue to raise the cultural context of a defendant's actions during trial and sentencing and it will be up to the court to decide what weight to attach to such arguments.

This Chapter has highlighted the main arguments for, and against, accepting cultural defences in domestic law and has underscored some difficulties when transplanting these arguments to the level of the ICC, particularly in the context of the influence of international human rights law. Another question that has arisen in a number of analyses of the cultural defence in domestic law is whether this defence should be available in cases involving 'irreparable harm'.[94] This is even more significant in the context of the ICC, which has jurisdiction over only the most serious of all international crimes;[95] genocide, crimes against humanity, war crimes and aggression.[96] The following Chapter discusses the nature and development of the ICC in more depth, in an attempt to see if cultural defences should be accepted before this Court.

Notes

1 See Alison Dundes Renteln, 'Making Room for Culture in the Court' (2010) 49 *The Judges Journal* 7, 7–15; Alison Dundes Renteln and Rene Valladares, 'The Importance of Culture for the Justice System' (2009) 92 *Judicature* 193; and Alison Dundes Renteln, 'The Use and Abuse of the Cultural Defense' (2005) 20 *Canadian Journal of Law and Society* 47.

2 Some States, particularly those with a multicultural population, make room for cultural considerations when drafting legislation, although such examples are limited. See Gordon R Woodman, 'The Culture Defence in English Common Law: the Potential for Development' in Marie-Claire Foblets and Alison Dundes Renteln (eds), *Multicultural Jurisprudence* (Hart Publishing 2009), 7, 16–17. In the UK, for example, the *Motor-Cycle Crash Helmets (Religious Exemption) Act 1976*, re-enacted in the *Road Traffic Act 1988* provides, in section 16(2) that the rules requiring motorcycle riders to wear a helmet 'shall not apply to any follower of the Sikh religion while he is wearing a turban', thus facilitating the Sikh religion requirement that men wear a turban at all times. Cultural issues also find a place in Canadian legislation in respect of sentencing. Section 718.2(e) of the Canadian Criminal Code, RSC 1985, c C-46 provides that 'all available sanctions other than imprisonment that are reasonable in the circumstances should be considered for all offenders, with particular attention to the circumstances of aboriginal offenders'.

3 See Dundes Renteln and Valladares (n 1), 197.

4 See Julia P Sams, 'The Availability of the "Cultural Defense" as an Excuse for Criminal Behavior' (1986) 16 *Georgia Journal of International and Comparative Law* 335; Jeroen Van Broeck, 'Cultural Defence and Culturally Motivated Crimes (Cultural Offences) (2001) 9(1) *European Journal of Crime, Criminal Law and Criminal Justice* 1; M-C Foblets, 'Cultural Delicts: The Repercussion of Cultural Conflicts on Delinquent Behaviour. Reflections on the Contribution of Legal Anthropology to a Contemporary Debate' (1998) 6 *European Journal of Crime, Criminal Law and Criminal Justice* 187; and Carolyn Choi, 'Application of a Cultural Defense in Criminal Proceedings' (1990) 8(1) *Pacific Basin Law Journal* 80.

5 See Van Broeck (n 4) and Thalia Anthony, Lorna Bartels and Anthony Hopkins, 'Lessons Lost in Sentencing: Welding Individualised Justice to Indigenous Justice' (2015) 39 *Melbourne University Law Review* 46.

6 Dundes Renteln and Valladares (n 1), 194.

7 *Ibid.*, 201. They comment that '[c]ulture shapes cognition and conduct in profound ways. Individuals are predisposed to act in certain ways based on their cultural conditioning. An understanding of the cultural background and motivation of the litigants is essential to properly gauge such fundamental issues as culpability and level of punishment deserved'.

8 *US v Bauer*, 84 F. 3d 1549 (9th Cir. Ct, 1996).

9 See John Rhodes, 'Up in Smoke: The Religious Freedom Restoration Act and Federal Marijuana Prosecutions' (2015) 38 *Oklahoma City University Law Review* 319.

10 Nuotio comments that '[c]ultural sensitivity deserves attention. Cultural grounds have a role to play in criminal proceedings, but these should find a role in the frame of the ordinary criminal law doctrines'. Kimmo Nuotio, 'Between Denial

and Recognition: Criminal Law and Cultural Diversity' in Will Kymlicka, Claes Lernestedt and Matt Matravers (eds), *Criminal Law and Cultural Diversity* (Oxford University Press 2014), 85, 86.

11 N. A-091133 (Los Angeles Super. Ct. 1985) (unpublished opinion). See Dundes Renteln and Valladares (n 1), 194.

12 See *ibid.*, 194.

13 *R v Ipeelee* [2012] 1 SCR 433, 469 [60].

14 With regard to the abuse of the cultural defence, see the case of Adelaide Abankwah, who made a false claim concerning the threat of female genital mutilation, when seeking political asylum in the US. See Dundes Renteln (2005) (n 1), 57.

15 Will Kymlicka, Claes Lernestedt and Matt Matravers, 'Introduction: Criminal Law and Cultural Diversity' in Will Kymlicka, Claes Lernestedt and Matt Matravers (eds), *Criminal Law and Cultural Diversity* (Oxford University Press 2014), 1, 5.

16 Woodman (n 2), 8.

17 Barrie Sander, 'The Expressive Limits of International Criminal Justice: Victim Trauma and Local Culture in the Iron Cage of the Law' (2016) iCourts Working Paper Series, No 38 2016 https://papers.ssrn.com/sol3/papers.cfm?abstract_id=2711236 accessed 2 October 2017, 14.

18 See definition put forward by the Canadian Commission for UNESCO, 'A Working Definition of "Culture"', (1977) 4 *Cultures* 78: 'Culture is a dynamic value system of learned elements, with assumptions, conventions, beliefs and rules permitting members of a group to relate to each other and to the world, to communicate and develop their creative potential.'

19 Committee on Economic, Social and Cultural Rights, General comment No. 21, Right of everyone to take part in cultural life (art. 15, para. 1 (a)), U.N. Doc. E/C.12/GC/21 (2009).

20 Kymlicka, Lernestedt and Matravers (n 15), 3, footnote 5.

21 Woodman states that '[t]he use of the adjective "cultural" in this context seems grammatically erroneous. "Cultural defence" should designate a defence which is an intrinsic part of a culture, just as a cultural dance and cultural antagonism are parts of cultures. In contrast, the present discussion is concerned with a defence which may exist with a legal system, not within a defendant's culture. It is a legal defence based upon culture. We refer similarly to the provocation defence, a legal defence based upon the fact of provocation of the defendant, and the defence of mistake, a legal defence based upon the fact that the defendant acted on the ground of a mistaken belief. If we speak of the cultural defence, we should refer to these as the provocative defence and the mistaken defence'. Woodman (n 2), 7, footnote 2.

22 Nuotio (n 10), 81.

23 Bhikhu Parekh, 'Cultural Defense and the Criminal Law' in Will Kymlicka, Claes Lernestedt and Matt Matravers (eds), *Criminal Law and Cultural Diversity* (Oxford University Press 2014), 104, 107–108.

24 *Ibid.*

25 Elsa Stamatopoulou, *The Right to Culture in International Law* (Brill 2007), 5.

26 *Ibid.*

27 *Ibid.*, 11–16.

28 Article 27 of the Universal Declaration of Human Rights Proclaimed by the United Nations General Assembly in Paris on 10 December 1948 (General

Assembly resolution 217 A). Article 27 states: '(1) Everyone has the right freely to participate in the cultural life of the community, to enjoy the arts and to share in scientific advancement and its benefits. (2) Everyone has the right to the protection of the moral and material interests resulting from any scientific, literary or artistic production of which he is the author.'

29 International Covenant on Civil and Political Rights. Adopted by the General Assembly of the United Nations on 19 December 1966.

30 Convention on the Elimination of All Forms of Discrimination against Women. Adopted and opened for signature, ratification and accession by General Assembly resolution 34/180 of 18 December 1979, entry into force 3 September 1981, in accordance with article 27(1).

31 Convention on the Rights of the Child. Adopted and opened for signature, ratification and accession by General Assembly resolution 44/25 of 20 November 1989, entry into force 2 September 1990, in accordance with article 49.

32 International Convention on the Protection of the Rights of All Migrant Workers and Members of Their Families. Adopted by General Assembly resolution 45/158 of 18 December 1990.

33 Declaration on the Rights of Persons Belonging to National or Ethnic, Religious and Linguistic Minorities Adopted by General Assembly resolution 47/135 of 18 December 1992.

34 See, for example, UNESCO Declaration on Cultural Diversity, adopted in 2001.

35 Indigenous and Tribal Peoples Convention 1989, No, 169.

36 African Charter on Human and Peoples' Rights 1982, OAU Doc. CAB/LEG/67/3 rev. 5. See Article 17.

37 Framework Convention for the Protection of National Minorities 1998, ETS No. 157.

38 Charter of Fundamental Rights of the European Union 2000. (2000/C 364/01).

39 Committee on Economic, Social and Cultural Rights, General Comment 21, Right of Everyone to Take Part in Cultural Life, 21 December 2009, E/C.12/GC/21, para 32.

40 Committee on Economic, Social and Cultural Rights, General Comment 21, Right of Everyone to Take Part in Cultural Life, 21 December 2009, E/C.12/GC/21, para 40.

41 Committee on Economic, Social and Cultural Rights, General Comment 21, Right of Everyone to Take Part in Cultural Life, 21 December 2009, E/C.12/GC/21, para 48.

42 Committee on Economic, Social and Cultural Rights, General Comment 21, Right of Everyone to Take Part in Cultural Life, 21 December 2009, E/C.12/GC/21, para 63.

43 See General Comment No. 23: The rights of minorities (Art. 27). (1994). CCPR/C/21/Rev.1/Add.5.

44 Alison Dundes Renteln, 'What Do We Have to Fear from Cultural Defense?' in Will Kymlicka, Claes Lernestedt and Matt Matravers (eds), *Criminal Law and Cultural Diversity* (Oxford University Press 2014), 175, 180.

45 *Ibid.*

46 The ICCPR has been ratified by 169 States and the ICESCR has been ratified by 165 States. See: http://indicators.ohchr.org/ accessed 2 October 2017.

47 However, both Article 15 of the ICESCR and Article 27 of the ICCPR reflect Article 27 of the UDHR, and it is generally accepted that this instrument is now part of the customary international law of nations and therefore binding

on all States. On the customary nature of the UDHR, see J Humphrey, 'The International Bill of Rights and Implementation: Scope and Implementation' (1976) 17 *William and Mary Law Review* 527.

48 See Jack Donnelly, 'Cultural Relativism and Universal Human Rights' (1984) 6 *Human Rights Quarterly* 400.

49 Stamatopoulou (n 24), 4.

50 International Convention on the Elimination of All Forms of Racial Discrimination. Adopted and opened for signature and ratification by General Assembly resolution 2106 (XX) of 21 December 1965.

51 Convention on the Elimination of All Forms of Discrimination against Women Adopted and opened for signature, ratification and accession by General Assembly Resolution 34/180 of 18 December 1979.

52 Convention on the Rights of the Child. Adopted and opened for signature, ratification and accession by General Assembly Resolution 44/25 of 20 November 1989.

53 Declaration on the Rights of Persons Belonging to National or Ethnic, Religious and Linguistic Minorities. A/RES/47. 92nd plenary meeting, 18 December 1992.

54 Declaration on the Elimination of Violence against Women. A/RES/48/104. 85th plenary meeting, 20 December 1993.

55 Stamatopoulou (n 24), 28.

56 See, for example, General Recommendation No. 14 of the CEDAW committee with regard to female genital mutilation. General Recommendation No 14. Adopted at the Ninth Session of the Committee on the Elimination of Discrimination against Women, in 1990. Contained in Document A/45/38 and Corrigendum. For an analysis of the work of human rights treaty monitoring bodies on the issue of cultural relativism, see, generally, Stamatopoulou (n 24).

57 UNESCO Universal Declaration on Cultural Diversity. Adopted by the General Conference, Paris, France, 2 November 2001.

58 Merriam-Webster Dictionary. Available at: www.merriam-webster.com/dictionary/ enculturation accessed 2 October.

59 Dundes Renteln and Valladares (n 1), 195.

60 Parekh (n 22), 108–109.

61 *Ibid.*, 109. Parekh comments: 'Cultural defense or an appeal to an individual's culture is not intended to absolve the agent of her responsibility for her action. Its purpose rather is to clarify the nature and meaning of her action, explain why she did it, and in some circumstances to provide a defense of it.'

62 Dundes Renteln and Valladares (n 1), 194. They state: '[i]t is difficult to overstate the importance of culture and the subtle pressure it exerts on individuals. Culture is pervasive and all-encompassing; it shapes perceptions and affects behavior in every society, even though individuals are largely unaware of these processes. Although culture influences individuals, this does not mean it determines human behavior. The most that can be said is that cultural imperatives predispose individuals to react to phenomena.'

63 Parekh (n 22), 113.

64 *Ibid.*, 109.

65 Stamatopoulou (n 24), 199.

66 Article 18 states: '1. Everyone shall have the right to freedom of thought, conscience and religion. This right shall include freedom to have or to adopt a religion or belief of his choice, and freedom, either individually or in community with others and in public or private, to manifest his religion or belief in worship, observance, practice and teaching. 2. No one shall be subject to coercion which

would impair his freedom to have or to adopt a religion or belief of his choice. 3. Freedom to manifest one's religion or beliefs may be subject only to such limitations as are prescribed by law and are necessary to protect public safety, order, health, or morals or the fundamental rights and freedoms of others. 4. The States Parties to the present Covenant undertake to have respect for the liberty of parents and, when applicable, legal guardians to ensure the religious and moral education of their children in conformity with their own convictions.' ICCPR, Adopted by the General Assembly of the United Nations on 19 December 1966.

67 Dundes Renteln (n 43), 179.

68 With regard to international human rights law, see Article 14 of the ICCPR.

69 Article 67 of the Rome Statute sets out the minimum rights of a defendant and reflects Article 14 of the ICCPR. This provision should be read with reference to other Rome Statute provisions, including Article 55, which deals with the rights of persons during investigations; Article 74, regarding the right to a reasoned judgment, and Article 21(3), which prescribes that the Statute is to be interpreted in the context of internationally recognised human rights treaties.

70 See Dundes Renteln (n 43), 180. She states that it 'is possible that this due process argument will appear to be the more compelling rationale for the official adoption of a cultural defense policy'.

71 Article 67 of the Rome Statute.

72 See Kumaralingam Amirthalingam, 'Culture, Crime and Culpability: Perspectives on the Defence of Provocation' in Marie-Claire Foblets and Alison Dundes Renteln (eds), *Multicultural Jurisprudence* (Hart Publishing 2009), 35, 43. He comments: 'there are several obstacles to the development of a cultural defence. It risks fragmenting the law and resulting in unequal treatment of individuals.'

73 Dundes Renteln (n 43), 181.

74 Anton-Hermann Chroust, 'Aristotle's Conception of Equality (Epieikeia)' (1942) 18(2) *Notre Dame Law Review* 119.

75 Barbara Truffin and César Arjona, 'The Cultural Defence in Spain' in Marie-Claire Foblets and Alison Dundes Renteln (eds), *Multicultural Jurisprudence* (Hart Publishing 2009), 85, 118.

76 Rome Statute 1998. Article 7(1)(h)of the Statute also includes, as a crime against humanity, persecution on cultural or religious grounds.

77 Larissa van den Herik, 'Economic, Social and Cultural Rights – International Criminal Law's Blind Spot?' in E Riedel, C Golay, C Mahon and G Giacca (eds) *Economic, Social and Cultural Rights: Contemporary Issues and Challenges* (Oxford: Oxford University Press, 2013), 343–368, 343.

78 *Ibid.*

79 Dundes Renteln (n 43), 179–180.

80 John L Caughey, 'The Anthropologist as Expert Witnesses: a Murder in Maine' in Marie-Claire Foblets and Alison Dundes Renteln (eds), *Multicultural Jurisprudence* (Hart Publishing 2009), 321, 326.

81 Parekh (n 22), 111–112.

82 *Ibid.*, 109.

83 See Anthony, Bartels and Hopkins (n 5); Sarah Krasnostein, 'Too Much Individualisation, Not Enough Justice' (2014) 39(1) *Alternative Law Journal* 12; and DL Coleman, 'Individualizing Justice through Multiculturalism: The Liberals' Dilemma' (1996) 96(5) *Columbia Law Review* 1093.

84 Anthony, Bartels and Hopkins (n 5), 51.

85 Parekh (n 22), 109.

86 See Dundes Renteln (2005) (n 1), 62. She states that courts 'must acknowledge the influence of cultural imperatives as part of individualized justice'.
87 See Anthony, Bartels and Hopkins (n 5).
88 Dundes Renteln (2005) (n 1), 62.
89 Woodman (n 2), 33. He states: 'It has been shown that, unless there is a radical legislative intervention, it is most unlikely that the common law of England will develop a culture defence as a distinct general exemption defence. Even if that were to be considered, there could be difficulties arising from the implications of the Human Rights Act 1998 and the possibility of incompatibility between the Act and a statute introducing a general culture defence if it have effect to aspects of cultures which were inimical to the observance of human rights.'
90 Dundes Renteln (2005) (n 1), 63.
91 Parekh (n 22), 113–114.
92 Amirthalingam (n 71), 37.
93 In support of his theory, Amirthalingam illustrates how the 'Battered Woman Syndrome' was developed by feminist scholars. This syndrome was not put forward as a separate defence, 'but was instead used to educate judges and juries of alternative realities in order to allow the existing doctrines to be applied fairly to battered women who kill'. *Ibid.*, 44–45.
94 Dundes Renteln (n 43), 183.
95 Article 5 of the Rome Statute sets out the crimes over which the ICC has jurisdiction.
96 The jurisdiction of the ICC over the crime of aggression has not yet been activated. See Dapo Akande, 'The ICC Assembly of States Parties Prepares to Activate the ICC's Jurisdiction over the Crime of Aggression: But Who Will be Covered by that Jurisdiction?' (*EJIL:Talk!*, 26 June 2017) www.ejiltalk.org/the-icc-assembly-of-states-parties-prepares-to-activate-the-iccs-jurisdiction-over-the-crime-of-aggression-but-who-will-be-covered-by-that-jurisdiction/ accessed 2 October 2017.

2 The ICC Statute: a culture clash?

Introduction

Established in 1998, the ICC is the first permanent court with jurisdiction over the most serious international crimes: genocide, crimes against humanity, war crimes and aggression.[1] Becoming a State Party to the Rome Statute requires States to accept a limitation to their sovereignty when crimes that are of concern to the international community as a whole are committed.[2] The fact that States have been willing to relinquish some of their rights to prosecute such crimes 'is extremely significant considering that criminal law has historically been the most self-contained part of a domestic justice system, constituting one of the most central expressions of the socio-cultural identity of a country'.[3] This is all the more significant, given that representatives from very different legal families and culturally diverse States negotiated, and compromised on, the rules and framework of this institution. These States, while advocating for rules that were familiar and identifiable to themselves, created a new institution with its own socio-cultural identity. When analysing the potential use of cultural defences at the ICC, therefore, we must query if the Court is indeed 'cultured'; and if so, which States / legal traditions influenced it, and consequently if this to the advantage or disadvantage of certain States / legal traditions?

This Chapter begins with a discussion of law as culture and cultured, and the implications of this in the context of international criminal tribunals. It then analyses the legal traditions and cultures that influenced the drafting of the Statue and questions whether the Statue accommodates all legal traditions and cultures. Finally, it discusses the sources of law set out in Article 21 of the Statute to ascertain whether cultural traditions could equate to 'general principles' and be regarded as applicable law.

Law as culture

Caughey comments that '[a] trial is a cultural ritual, crime a cultural construct, and the court a cultural apparatus that represents and enforces the dominant culture's values and perspectives'.[4] Linked to this, Kusters highlights that legal provisions are, therefore, not neutral, stating that 'rules governing jurisdiction and legislation are in fact already permeated with cultural presuppositions and of course in the final analysis law itself is culture'.[5] While this comment is made in respect of domestic legal systems, it also holds true in the context of international criminal law. Support for accepting cultural defences in criminal trials at the domestic level focuses, to a certain extent, on the argument that the legal system within a State is reflective, and indeed, resultant, of that State's culture. The drafters and interpreters of law are influenced by their background and understandings of the world. It is argued that law is, therefore 'cultured', and in multicultural States, criminal law rules are generally cultured 'to the advantage of the majority population'.[6] Therefore, in order to ensure that justice is done, it is incumbent on courts to take minority cultural values into consideration.[7] Transferring this issue to the international criminal law plane, do the same concerns hold true? International criminal law has developed significantly over the last 80 years and numerous courts and tribunals have been created to enforce it. However, international criminal law has been criticised as being 'a reflection of the hegemonic values of Western punitive criminal justice',[8] and as an imperialistic tool.[9] Chuter comments that 'international criminal justice [today] has a heavily Western, white, Anglo-Saxon character' and its 'vocabulary and concepts are not neutral . . . [but instead] are culturally specific, constructed and manipulated by a very small number of countries, most of which have English as their native or second language.'[10]

International criminal law has been utilised to respond to various serious violations of human rights and international humanitarian law in a number of places around the globe, including the former Yugoslavia, Rwanda and Sierra Leone. Courts in these locations have been analysed in respect of their cultural sensitivity by a number of authors.[11] While Bostian is quite positive with regard to the International Criminal Tribunal for Rwanda (ICTR) stating that it 'appropriately adopted a mild cultural relativist approach in its proceedings by considering cultural differences when evaluating witness testimony, interpreting the definition of certain crimes within the context of the Rwandan experience, and considering Rwandan sentencing practices when sentencing defendants,'[12] Wald highlights some cultural insensitivity problems with the International Criminal Tribunal for the former Yugoslavia (ICTY), commenting that the tribunal

> tries suspects in a country to which they have no ties and sentences them to prison in other foreign countries. To many internationalists this may reflect a triumph, but there are also voices urging caution . . . Our judicial systems, with their peculiar rights and remedies, are products and reflections of our unique political and cultural notions.[13]

In a similar vein to Wald, Kelsall underscores the failings of judges hearing child recruitment cases at the Special Court for Sierra Leone, stating:

> Immersed as they were in the precepts of international law, they were oblivious to another very powerful reason for thinking that the defendants could not have foreseen that their actions were punishable: namely, the cultural context in which they operated.[14]

The question arises, therefore, if the ICC can avoid some of the pitfalls experienced by earlier international criminal law tribunals and adequately address cultural concerns.

The making of the Rome Statute

A plan to create a permanent international criminal court dates back many years.[15] In the aftermath of World War II, a proposal for a permanent world criminal court was submitted to the General Assembly of the United Nations.[16] While the International Law Commission worked on the proposal during the twentieth century, the idea only really gained traction after the Cold War and once the *ad hoc* tribunals had been set up.[17] The ICC was established as a result of lengthy negotiations between a large number of States. Delegates to the United Nations Diplomatic Conference of Plenipotentiaries on the Establishment of an international Criminal Court, representing the major legal families of the world, voted overwhelmingly in favour of the ICC on 17 July 1998, with 120 votes in favour, four votes against and 21 abstentions.[18]

It is generally accepted that there are three major legal families, i.e. civil law, common law and Islamic law.[19] In 1998, the distribution of domestic legal families was as follows: 51% civil law states, 25% common law states, 14% Islamic law States, and 10% mixed law States,[20] which have elements of two or more legal traditions. Delegates at the Rome Conference were logically representing their own State interests, and pushed for the adoption of rules that were familiar in their domestic legal system, as '[l]egal training within each domestic legal tradition determines in part lawyers' understanding of basic legal concepts'.[21] This was not unique to the Rome Conference, as highlighted by Combs, who states: 'States have traditionally been rather chauvinistic about their own criminal justice systems and suspicious of foreign systems.'[22] This suspicion was more evident when negotiating the Rome Statute however, because

> criminal law is not merely a series of technical legal issues. It is most closely related to the society as a whole and depends to a great extent upon the acceptance of the people. It is part of the legal culture and the expression of what people are used to and what they expect.[23]

If the international court is familiar in structure, framework and rules, then States can be more comfortable with it and more confident about its decisions.[24]

Bohlander states that '[i]n practice ... the dichotomy of "common *v.* civil law" has been the dominant paradigm for the systemic conversation in international courts and tribunals. . .',[25] and, indeed, powerful States, representing both common law (also known as adversarial) and civil law (also known as inquisitorial) jurisdictions had significant impact on the drafting process of the Rome Statute. What emerged from the negotiations was a compromise document, which heavily reflects the common law tradition, but with some civil law elements, particularly in relation to the rules concerning procedure and evidence, but Islamic law did not have much of an influence on the negotiation process. All 22 Arab states were present during the drafting of the Rome Statute, as well as observer delegations from Palestine, the League of Arab States, the African Union and the Organization of the Islamic Conference. However, reflecting the spread of the three major legal systems, the number of Islamic law States negotiating at the Rome Conference was not as large as those representing common law and civil law traditions. In addition, there were some difficulties to be seen in the negotiations between delegations from Islamic law States and those from other jurisdictions as there were several political and cultural differences between them. In general, domestic criminal laws in most Islamic law States contrast significantly with international criminal law,[26] as this is a religion-based legal system.[27] Bassiouni, who was the chairman of the drafting Committee at the Rome Conference, comments that Arab Islamic law States have generally failed to adopt

> a progressive codification of Islamic criminal justice (procedure and administration), which could sift through and distil the law and practices of Islam and adapt it to a contemporary framework which would keep faith with the past, while setting the foundation for the future.[28]

These factors 'ultimately minimized the impact of the Islamic legal tradition on the structure and procedures of the ICC'.[29]

However, an understanding of Islamic law is very important at the ICC because, as stated by Badar, it 'is a particularly instructive example of a "sacred law" and differs from other systems so significantly that its study is indispensable in order to appreciate adequately the full range of possible legal phenomena'.[30] In addition, it is the law applicable in a number of situations that have come before the Court, and an appreciation of the Islamic legal tradition by the Court would be to the benefit of defendants, victims and the Court itself. However, it seems that the Court has only been influenced by civil and common law States and these traditions have moulded its legal cultural identity. It is important, therefore, to query if, and to what extent, the Court leaves room for other cultures to be accommodated and facilitated within its framework.

Cultural accommodation at the ICC

The Preamble of the Rome Statute states: 'Conscious that all peoples are united by common bonds, their cultures pieced together in a shared heritage, and concerned that this delicate mosaic may be shattered at any time. . .'[31] Christensen states that this language

> reflects the foundation and impetus for the establishment of the ICC. Building upon a common heritage for the establishment of peace is a noble and praiseworthy goal. However, just as the commonality of our heritages and cultures motivate the establishment of a permanent international criminal tribunal, the differences in our traditions encourage the voice of reason and caution to raise itself among the shouts of support for the International Criminal Court.[32]

The ICC does accommodate differences in cultures and does encourage respect for culture in its legal framework and procedures, although it does not include an explicit right to raise cultural defences. This section reviews the Rome Statute's provisions that seek to encourage and facilitate cultural accommodation and sensitivity and recognise the importance of culture.

Cultural property

The importance of culture to the ICC is illustrated through its provisions relating to cultural property. Articles 8(2)(b)(ix) and (e)(iv) of the Rome Statute criminalise attacks directed against cultural property (i.e. 'buildings dedicated to religion, education, art, science or charitable purposes, historic monuments, hospitals and places where the sick and wounded are collected, provided they are not military objectives'), both in international armed conflicts and non-international armed conflicts, as war crimes.[33] These provisions illustrate that the ICC is concerned with the protection of culture and the Court's approach to this protection will be analysed in Chapter 4 in the analysis of the case of *Prosecutor v Al Mahdi*, which focused on the destruction of mausoleums and religious sites during the non-international armed conflict in Mali. However, it is to be noted that attacks against cultural property are criminalised as war crimes only and not as crimes against humanity or as evidence of acts of genocide.[34] Given the current disturbing

trend of destruction of cultural sites by Islamic fundamentalist groups in
Syria, Iraq and Mali, as attacks upon the identity of minority groups, it is
suggested that the Court, if faced with cases of destruction of cultural property, should take a more expansive interpretation of the motivations behind
such attacks.[35]

Linguistic diversity[36]

One of the few cultural issues to consistently find a space in international
criminal trials to date has been the issue of linguistic diversity. This is
reflected in provisions of international tribunals that provide for defendants to have the right to an interpreter, and is recognised as an essential
element of the right to a fair trial in international human rights law.[37] This
aspect of the right to a fair trial is even more important at international
criminal tribunals, given the complexity of the proceedings, the gravity of
the accusations, and the 'foreign' nature of the court. In such circumstances,
it would be difficult enough even for a native speaker to understand all
aspects of the various substantive and procedural issues.[38] At the *ad hoc*
tribunals, Language Services Sections were established to address linguistic
rights.[39] At the ICC, the linguistic challenges are many, given its extensive
jurisdictional, and therefore, linguistic, reach.[40] The official languages of
the Court are Arabic, Chinese, English, French, Russian and Spanish,[41] with
the working languages being French and English.[42] However, the Court can
authorise a party to use a different language if so requested by any party to
a proceeding or by a State allowed to intervene in a proceeding, if this is
justified.[43] Lawyers and judges at the ICC must be proficient in at least one
of the languages of the Court.[44] In addition, the right to an interpreter for
the defendant[45] must be facilitated and the linguistic needs of witnesses, and
affected communities, must also be accommodated.[46] All of these needs are
overseen by the Language Services Section of the ICC.

The linguistic challenges in the ICC have been described by Diederick
Zanen, head of the Field and Operational Interpretation Unit in the ICC
Registry. He states:

> At the ICC, for every case different languages are relevant because it's
> a different country and it's a different situation. For example, in Kenya,
> people may speak Swahili, or Luhya or Kikuyu. In Côte d'Ivoire they
> speak Jula or Bambara or French, or another local language. In the
> Central African Republic, Sango is an important language. In Libya,
> they are going to speak Arabic. All the languages change, which means
> that the requirements are different for each case. That's why we have
> very little—there's only staff for those languages in cases that are either

at the trial stage or for languages that are needed for a longer duration, languages that are widely spoken, that may be relevant to several cases. A lot of the languages that I work with now are only relevant to one situation country or maybe even unique to one case, or maybe even for one or two witnesses.[47]

Linguistic challenges do not relate only to the narrow translation or inter-pretation of words, however, as language comes with its own cultural context. Therefore, proficiency in a language may not be enough to fully understand the meaning of phrases and words. This problem was identified in the ICTR in a number of cases.[48] In the case of *Akayesu*, for example, the Trial Chamber acknowledged the existence of 'cultural factors which might affect an understanding of the evidence presented'.[49] The Trial Chamber noted the difficulty in translating evidence from witnesses who spoke Kinyarwanda, because its grammar and colloquial expressions were diffi-cult to translate into the official languages of the tribunal. The Chamber also noted other cultural factors that influenced the translation of witness testi-mony in this case, i.e. Rwandans have an oral tradition and normally report events as if they have seen them themselves, even if they have only heard about them.[50] An expert witness in linguistics, Dr Mathias Ruzindana, gave evidence at the Tribunal and stated that 'in ascertaining the specific meaning of certain words and expressions in Kinyarwanda, it is necessary to place them contextually, both in time and space'.[51] Also before the ICTR, in the case of *Rutaganda*, the Trial Chamber acknowledged that it had considered 'various social and cultural factors in assessing the testimony of the wit-nesses', including their level of education, which had caused them difficulty 'in testifying as to dates, times, distances, colours and motor vehicles'.[52] Similarly, in the case of *Musema*, the ICTR Trial Chamber stated that it had not drawn negative inferences as to the credibility of witnesses who were unfamiliar with 'spatio-temporal identification mechanisms and techniques'.[53] It is clear from these cases that it is necessary for international criminal courts and tribunals to seek the opinion of linguistic and socio-linguistic experts to explain the culture behind the language, where necessary, and not just facilitate interpretation, in order to ensure a fair trial.

Victims and witnesses

The Rome Statute requires cultural sensitivity with regard to victims and witnesses.[54] Under the Rules of Procedure and Evidence of the ICC, the Victims and Witnesses Unit has responsibility to ensure 'training of its staff with respect to victims' and witnesses' security, integrity and dignity, including matters related to gender and cultural sensitivity'.[55] Furthermore, this Unit 'may include, as appropriate, persons with expertise in (e) gender and cultural diversity'.[56] The exact parameters of this provision are unclear, but it underscores the fact that the Court is aware of cultural diversity challenges concerning victims and witnesses, and that their culture should be respected by the Court.

Expert witnesses on cultural issues[57]

While the Regulations of the Court do not specifically mention cultural witnesses, Article 44 of the Regulations mentions expert witnesses,[58] which could include experts on cultural practices and traditions. Evidence of such witnesses could aid the Court by elucidating elements of cultural practices and commenting on the enculturation process. Court Regulation 44.1 states:

> The Registrar shall create and maintain a list of experts accessible at all times to all organs of the Court and to all participants. Experts shall be included on such a list following an appropriate indication of expertise in the relevant field

and according to Regulation 44.5

> [t]he Chamber may issue any order as to the subject of an expert report, the number of experts to be instructed, the mode of their instruction, the manner in which their evidence is to be presented and the time limits for the preparation and notification of their report.[59]

Over 200 experts have agreed to have their name included on the ICC website's List of Experts as of 18 August 2015.[60] The range of expertise spans many fields, including ballistics, forensic psychology, linguistics, psychiatry, psychology, with a handful of experts working in the fields of anthropology and history who could attest to cultural issues. The vast majority of these experts are, however, from Western States, particularly France and Australia.

The Regulations of the Court allow for the Trial Chamber to 'direct the joint instruction of an expert by the participants',[61] and allow the Court to issue any order 'in the interests of justice' concerning the 'joint or separate instruction' by the parties of expert witnesses.[62] In a status conference in the *Lubanga* case, the Chamber declared that 'the Chamber favours, where possible, the joint instruction of expert witnesses'.[63] The Chamber held that if the parties to the case were unable to agree on a joint instruction of an agreed-upon expert, then a separate instruction was possible. If separate instructions were given to the expert, he / she must prepare a single report, taking into account those differing instructions. The Chamber also held that the legal representatives of victims were entitled to contribute to a joint or separate instruction of the expert witness.[64]

Expert witnesses can help to mitigate against the abuse of the cultural defence by testifying to the cultural traditions in differ cultures and communities. Claims by defendants as to their actions being based on, or emanating from, a particular culture can be analysed better once evidence as to the defendant's culture is provided. Dundes Renteln comments that '[a] risk of misusing cultural defences certainly exists, and courts should adopt policies to try to avoid this risk'. She comments that expert witness on cultural issues should be sought by the Court '[t]o minimize the introduction of fraudulent arguments'.[65] The Trial Chamber may rule on the admissibility and relevance of any expert evidence and once that testimony is admitted, the expert witness may be questioned by the party instructing him, the opposing party, or the Chamber.[66]

There are, however, no certification policies with regard to expert witnesses, a fact that is flagged by Dundes Renteln as in need of change. She states that '[a] carefully designed credentialing system will allow for the institutional guarantee of an expert's credentials and ensure that the expert possesses the requisite knowledge in the relevant field'.[67] Such a move would be welcome to ensure the veracity of cultural claims before the Court.

Judges

According to Article 36(8) of the Rome Statute, the selection of ICC judges is based on: representation of the principal legal systems of the world; equitable geographical representation; and a fair representation of female and male judges. According to Article 36(4)(b), each State Party may put forward one candidate for any given election who need not necessarily be a national of that State Party but shall in any case be a national of a State Party. The ICC distinguishes between judges who have criminal law backgrounds and those who have international law backgrounds. Article 36 of the Rome Statute requires that every candidate for election to the role of judge have an expertise in either criminal law or international law.[68] Article 39 sets out the rules in respect of the expertise of judges in the Chambers. This states:

> The assignment of judges to divisions shall be based on the nature of the functions to be performed by each division and the qualification and experience of the judges elected to the Court, in such a way that each division shall contain an appropriate combination of expertise in criminal law and procedure and in international law. The Trial and Pre-Trial Divisions shall be composed predominantly of judges with criminal trial experience.[69]

It is important that Chambers include a mix of legal traditions, but it is also important that Chambers are open to dealing appropriately and in depth with foreign concepts and traditions. As mentioned earlier, Kelsall highlighted a number of problems with child recruitment cases at the Special Court for Sierra Leone. Evidence was heard about superstitions and magic concerning the recruitment of child soldiers, who felt that they became bullet proof through an initiation ceremony conducted by the accused. The Court, Kelsall states, 'proved deaf to an enormously important system of local magical belief' and 'drew on an unrealistic Western norm'.[70] It is, therefore, important, that judges are open to cultural contexts that are significantly different to their own and that they do not dismiss or ignore practices rooted in culture. If they simply sidestep or ignore such cultural traditions, then the Court will be in danger of losing legitimacy in the eyes of many.

Sentencing

Article 76 of the Rome Statute provides that if a defendant is found guilty, it is left to the Trial Chamber to determine an 'appropriate sentence'.[71] In doing so, 'it shall take into account the evidence presented and submissions made during the trial that are relevant to the sentence'.[72] The possible penalties are set out in Article 77, being imprisonment for a specified number of years, which may not exceed a maximum of 30 years or, when justified by the gravity of the office, a term of life imprisonment. In addition to imprisonment, the Court may order that a fine be paid or goods forfeited.[73]

The Chamber is given some guidance with regard to sentencing in both the Statute and the Rules of Procedure and Evidence, but there is no detailed sentencing template, thus giving the Chamber significant discretion. Article 78 of the Statute provides that in determining the sentence, the Court shall 'take into account such factors as the gravity of the crime and the individual circumstances of the convicted person'.[74] Rule 145 of the Rules of Procedure and Evidence supplements this provision, and provides additional guidance to the Chamber in respect of sentencing, stating that the Court shall:

> (a) Bear in mind that the totality of any sentence of imprisonment and fine, as the case may be, imposed under article 77 must reflect the culpability of the convicted person; (b) Balance all the relevant factors, including any mitigating and aggravating factors and consider the circumstances both of the convicted person and of the crime; (c) In addition to the factors mentioned in article 78, paragraph 1, give consideration, inter alia, to the extent of the damage caused, in particular the harm caused to the victims and their families, the nature of the unlawful behaviour and the means employed to execute the crime; the

degree of participation of the convicted person; the degree of intent; the circumstances of manner, time and location; and the age, education, social and economic condition of the convicted person.[75]

The Statute then sets out a number of aggravating and mitigating factors, which the Court 'shall take into account, as appropriate'.[76] The Prosecutor must establish aggravating factors beyond a reasonable doubt, while the defendant must prove mitigating circumstances on the balance of probabilities. The mitigating factors are

> (i) The circumstances falling short of constituting grounds for exclusion of criminal responsibility, such as substantially diminished mental capacity or duress; (ii) The convicted person's conduct after the act, including any efforts by the person to compensate the victims and any cooperation with the Court.[77]

The aggravating factors comprise

> (i) Any relevant prior criminal convictions for crimes under the jurisdiction of the Court or of a similar nature; (ii) Abuse of power or official capacity; (iii) Commission of the crime where the victim is particularly defenceless; (iv) Commission of the crime with particular cruelty or where there were multiple victims; (v) Commission of the crime for any motive involving discrimination on any of the grounds referred to in article 21, paragraph 3; (vi) Other circumstances which, although not enumerated above, by virtue of their nature are similar to those mentioned.[78]

Clearly, the cultural background of the defendant can be taken into consideration under these provisions. Rule 145 allows for 'the circumstances of manner, time, and location; and the age, education, social and economic condition of the convicted person' to be considered when sentencing. In addition, the Article 78 phrasing of 'the individual circumstances of the convicted person'[79] allows the cultural context of the defendant's actions to be taken into account. The phrasing of Rule 145(2)(a) leaves room for consideration of 'circumstances falling short of constituting grounds for exclusion of criminal responsibility',[80] which may also allow for the cultural context to be considered.

The sentencing may take place at a distinct phase of the trial, if either party requests it, or if the Court decides that it should, thus allowing for extra evidence, not submitted at trial to be considered in respect of sentencing.[81] This new evidence could include evidence in respect of the cultural motivations of the defendant.

The lack of sentencing guidelines at the ICC and other international tribunals has been discussed by a number of authors, and various opinions put forward as to how judges at international criminal trials should come to sentencing decisions. Schabas, for example, suggests that sentencing at international trials be guided by human rights principles, which focus on rehabilitative rather than retributive goals.[82] Such an approach may include a focus on a person's culture, given the protection of the right to culture in numerous international human rights instruments. However, there are a variety of other approaches to sentencing espoused by other authors,[83] including those based on retributive norms,[84] expressive notions of punishment,[85] and general deterrence.[86]

In contrast to these authors who presume that there exists a thing that is 'international criminal sentencing', Combs argues that such a thing does, and should, not exist. Instead, she proposes that consideration of domestic sentencing norms at international trials provides international courts with 'valuable benefits, most notably in increased legitimacy for the international courts' own sentences'.[87] The sentencing provisions of the ICTY and the ICTR allow the tribunals to 'have recourse to the general practice regarding prison sentences' in the States in which the crime was perpetrated,[88] however such an approach was not always adhered to by the tribunals.[89] In the case of *Ruggiu* before the ICTR, the Chamber took the Rwandan criminal law's categorisation of perpetrators of genocide or crimes against humanity into consideration. The Chamber noted that it was not required to follow Rwandan sentencing practice, but that it was obliged to 'take account' of such practice.[90]

During negotiations on the sentencing provisions for the Rome Statute, the idea of considering domestic norms was proposed, and was favoured by Middle Eastern States.[91] However, this approach was rejected, with those against the idea arguing that taking consideration of domestic law 'would allow for different regimes of penalties to be applied by the Court and would mean the application of a discriminatory system of sanctions'.[92] Rejecting a need for universal sentencing norms, which have been called for by some commentators,[93] Combs contends 'that efforts to develop universal sentencing norms are far less likely to result in shared global norms as they are to result in the adoption of Western norms over the objections of non-Western stake-holders'.[94] While not framed within a specific 'cultural' argument, Combs' proposal that international courts 'afford domestic sentencing laws substantial and demonstrable influence on an international court's sentencing scheme unless countervailing considerations require it to play a lesser role'[95] is in line with cultural concerns regarding international courts. As one of her justifications for this opinion, she underscores the potential lack of credibility of a Court when there is a disconnect between international sentencing provisions and domestic sentencing norms, and the latter are created and shaped by the culture of the State in which they are adopted. However, the importance of consistency and predictability in sentencing and in international criminal law cannot be overlooked, and whether the Court would be willing to make such a bold move is doubtful.

The Court can address cultural issues when deciding on where the guilty person will serve his sentence, and try to ensure that the place of incarceration would facilitate some of their cultural practices. Article 103 of the Statute provides that a 'sentence of imprisonment shall be served in a State designated by the Court from a list of States which have indicated to the Court their willingness to accept sentenced persons'.[96] To this end, the Court has entered into Agreements on the Enforcement of Sentences with the International Criminal Court with a number of States, whereby a state agrees to carry out a sentence imposed by the Court. In addition, some States have declared their willingness to accept their own nationals or, in some cases, their residents, to serve a sentence imposed by the Court on their territory. A number of States have added the additional condition that the sentence cannot exceed the maximum time allowed for a sentence under national law.[97] States can also enter an *ad hoc* agreement with the Court, such as those signed by the Democratic Republic of the Congo in respect of Germain Katanga[98] and Thomas Lubanga Dyilo, allowing these nationals to serve the final portion of their sentence in prisons in the DRC.[99] Serving a sentence in one's own State or in a State with a similar culture would be the optimum situation and would illustrate the Court's willingness to be culturally sensitive.

Reparations

One of the main aims of the Rome Statute is to address the needs of victims of the most serious crimes. One of the ways in which this is facilitated is via the Reparations procedure set out in the Statute. Article 75 of the Statute provides the Court with the authority to order reparations directly to, or in respect of, victims.[100] As with the sentencing hearing, a hearing on reparations can be held as a distinct phase of the trial.[101] Reparations can take the form of restitution, compensation, and / or rehabilitation. According to Rule 94 of the Rules of Procedure and Evidence, a victim's request for reparations under article 75 shall contain a number of details, including a description of the injury, loss or harm. Article 75 provides that before making a reparations order that the 'Court may invite and shall take account of representations from or on behalf of the convicted person, victims, other interested persons or interested States'.[102] The Court can assess the quantity and quality of damage done to victims. In this context cultural issues can be considered. In this case, however, it is the impact on the victims' culture that is at issue, rather than that of the defendant. As will be analysed in Chapter 4, the ICC decision on reparations in the *Al Mahdi* case focused, to a significant extent, on the impact of the destruction of mausoleums and religious sites on the cultural life of Timbuktu.

Article 21 of the ICC Statute and sources of law: a cultural portal?

While it is clear from the above discussion that the ICC legal framework leaves room for cultural considerations explicitly, it is also important to question if the Court can draw on domestic law concerning cultural practices in coming to their decisions. The ICC can have recourse to a number of sources when deciding a legal issue, some of which may allow for a greater understanding of the cultural context of the actions of the defendants. These sources are set out in Article 21 of the Rome Statute, which has been described as 'a tissue of imperfectly defined sources'.[103] Article 21 modifies the approach taken to sources of law in Article 38 of the Statute of the International Court of Justice 'to fit the context of international *criminal* law'.[104] Article 21 states:

1   The Court shall apply:

   (a) In the first place, this Statute, Elements of Crimes and its Rules of Procedures and Evidence;
   (b) In the second place, where appropriate, applicable treaties and the principles and rules of international law, including the established principles of the international law of armed conflict;
   (c) Failing that, general principles of law derived by the Court from national laws of legal systems of the world including, as appropriate, the national laws of States that would normally exercise jurisdiction over the crime, provided that those principles are not inconsistent with this Statute and with international law and internationally recognized norms and standards.

2   The Court may apply principles and rules of law as interpreted in its previous decisions.
3   The application and interpretation of law pursuant to this article must be consistent with internationally recognized human rights, and be without any adverse distinction founded on grounds such as gender as defined in article 7, paragraph 3, age, race, colour, language, religion, or belief, political or other opinion, national, ethnic or social origin, wealth, birth or other status.

Article 21, unlike Article 38 of the ICJ Statute, establishes a clear and strict hierarchy between sources, and is, thus, more rigid. There is little room for cultural issues to be raised within the context of the ICC Statute, Elements of Crimes and Rules of Procedure and Evidence under Article 21(1)(a). However, paragraphs (b) and (c) may allow some flexibility for cultural considerations to be raised and accommodated.

Applicable treaties and the principles and rules of international law, including the established principles of the international law of armed conflict

Paragraph (b) allows the Court to have recourse to international law treaties, principles and rules, as a source of law. It has been asserted that international law is, however, essentially a Western construct, reflecting Western ideals and culture and may, therefore, be culturally biased. Picker states that

> although international law is global, upon examination it appears to be solidly within the Western legal tradition. This is not to suggest that international law has not grown in other regions and at other times in the absence of the Western legal tradition.[105]

He continues, stating '[i]t is usually asserted that international law is Western, though this is more a claim of Western control and direction of the development and institutions of international law than of the inherent character of international law'.[106] The nature of international law as a Western construct[107] has been highlighted by the Third World Approaches to International Law (TWAIL) school of critical legal scholarship, which

> rejects the traditional tenets and assumptions of traditional international law and argues for a re-imagination of the law of nations to purge it of racial and hegemonic precepts and biases to create a truly universal corpus that embraces inclusivity and empowerment.[108]

International human rights law has come in for significant criticism as representative of Western, and Christian, values. This has been manifested in the rejection of the Universal Declaration of Human Rights (UDHR)[109] in favour of the Universal Islamic Declaration of Human Rights,[110] adopted in 1981, by Islamic Councils in London and Paris. Similar documents, underscoring the Christian nature of the UDHR, which were subsequently adopted, include the Draft Charter on Human and People's Rights in the Arab World, endorsed by the Arab Union of Lawyers in 1987,[111] the Cairo Declaration on Human Rights in Islam, adopted by the Organisation of the

Islamic Conference in 1990,[112] and the Arab Charter on Human Rights, which was adopted by the League of Arab States in 2004.[113]

However, UN human rights instruments are open for ratification by all UN member States, and States can choose not to ratify instruments that are not in line with their ideals, or, indeed, make reservations to specific treaty provisions.[114] Therefore, the human rights instruments discussed in the previous Chapter, which contain provisions dealing with issues of culture and religion, including the ICCPR and the ICESCR, can be utilised as a source by the Court. Therefore, cultural issues could be considered by the Court, if they rely on Article 21(1)(b). This could, in theory, support the claim to raise cultural defences before the Court.

General principles of law[115]

'General principles of law' have been utilised as a source of public international law by international tribunals, since the adoption of the Statute of the Permanent Court of International Justice in 1920, to fill gaps in international law with regard to issues on which no rules exist. In any system of law, a situation may arise where a court realises that there is no rule covering the exact issue that has been raised.[116] Article 38 of the Statute of the International Court of Justice (ICJ) takes a similar approach, as does Article 21(1)(c) of the Rome Statute. Despite many international tribunals having recourse to general principles when identifying applicable law, significant uncertainty surrounds this source of law. In particular, uncertainty persists with regard to how general principles are to be identified and which techniques should be used to identify general principles. However, what is important to note is that the aim of the 'general principles' source of law is to identify a principle of international law based on a review of the domestic law of States with different legal and cultural backgrounds. It is accepted that in order for a principle of domestic law to be acknowledged as a general principle of international law, it must be recognised by most, but not all, legal systems of the world.[117] It is important that different legal families and cultures are represented, to mitigate against claims of a Westernised Court.

Raimondo states that

> the undeveloped nature of international criminal law, the imprecision of many of its legal rules, the need to make compelling legal arguments, and the existence of relevant domestic criminal law analogies have facilitated resort to and the subsequent application of general principles of law by international criminal courts and tribunals.[118]

However, there is no explicit reference to sources of law in the founding instruments of the first international criminal tribunals, i.e. the Charter of the International Military Tribunal[119] or the Charter of the International Military Tribunal for the Far East.[120] Moreover, none of the statutes of the hybrid tribunals, such as the Special Court for Sierra Leone,[121] the Extraordinary Chambers in the Courts of Cambodia,[122] or the Special Tribunal for Lebanon,[123] mention applicable law. Similarly, when the ICTY[124] and ICTR[125] were set up in the 1990s, no reference was made to sources of law in their statutes. Rather, these tribunals used Article 38 of the ICJ Statute as their guide to applicable law. The ICTY recognised that when its Statute was silent on a particular matter, it could refer to the other sources of law set out in the ICJ statute, including general principles.[126] Despite initial reluctance, both the ICTY and the ICTR have utilised domestic laws to help them to identify the applicable law.[127] The practice of the *ad hoc* and hybrid tribunals has been inconsistent when utilising general principles as a source of law. While these tribunals have recognised the need to resort to general principles in the absence of a treaty or customary rule, they have failed to develop a coherent practice when identifying such principles.[128]

The importance of general principles as a source of international criminal law was recognised by the drafters of the Rome Statute in Article 21 and this constitutes the first codification of the sources of international criminal law.[129] As with Article 38 of the ICJ Statute, Article 21(1)(c) seeks to avoid situations of *non liquet*, but judges can have recourse to general principles of law only when the sources set out in Article 21(1)(a) and Article 21(1)(b) have failed to identify a rule,[130] and indeed, so long as the general principle is in line with the human rights requirements set out in Article 21(3). Pellet states that this provision confers 'a wide discretionary power'[131] on the ICC judges and Danilenko states that the provision 'will provide ample opportunities for judicial creativity'.[132] Article 21(1)(c) does, indeed, provide room for judges to be creative, but identifying a general principle is a complex and difficult task. Whether the ICC would be willing to identify a principle based on culture remains to be seen.

According to Cassese, a principle of criminal law will fall within the parameters of Article 21(1)(c) of the Statute

> if a court finds that it is shared by common law and civil law systems as well as other legal systems such as those of the Islamic world, some Asian countries such as China and Japan, and the African continent.[133]

Pellet, however, is doubtful as to whether many legal cultures will be consulted in a review of national law in an attempt to identify general principles, stating that, in reality, the legal systems that will be consulted by the Court will be 'reduced to a small number in the contemporary world: the family of civil-law countries, the common law, and perhaps, Islamic law'.[134]

Article 21(c) contains a special reference to national laws of States that would normally exercise jurisdiction. Schabas states that this reference is intriguing because 'it suggests that the law applied by the Court might vary slightly depending on the place of the crime or the nationality of the offender'.[135] However, this will only happen once the legal systems of the world had been reviewed to find a consensus on a particular legal question. For example, in the context of a war crime in a non-international armed conflict in State X, perpetrated by a national of State X on a victim of State X, where no international law rule exists on a particular legal question, recourse could be had to the domestic law of State X to find the applicable law. However, if we substitute State Y for State X in the above example and State Y is a civil law country, while State X is a common law country, then the law of State Y could apply. This could lead to a situation where the law applied in a case, and perhaps, the outcome of the case, would differ as a result of the location of the crime, and the legal culture of that State. This is similar to Comb's argument of having recourse to domestic laws on sentencing discussed above. De Guzman comments that this 'particularized approach would undermine the consistent application of the law to different accused',[136] but that danger may be averted through the exercise of the Court's discretion to decide when it is 'appropriate' to refer to particular national laws.[137] However, the possibility still exists that the law of one State, based on its culture, may be found to be the applicable law in a case before the ICC.

Early jurisprudence of the court does indeed stress the subsidiary nature of Article 21(1)(c), however. In *Al Bashir*, the Court held that Article 21(1) (b) and (c) can only be applied if there is a lacuna in the written law in the Statute, the Elements of Procedure and Crimes and the Rules and in addition if this lacuna cannot be filled by applying the criteria set out in Articles 31 and 32 of the Vienna Convention of the Law of Treaties and Article 21(3) of the Rome Statute.[138] In the *Lubanga* case,[139] the ICC highlighted the exceptional nature of Article 21(1)(c) and undertook a rigorous and extensive review of national laws in its search for a general principle of law 'allowing the reviewability of decisions of an [*sic*] hierarchically lower court disallowing an appeal to a higher Court'. Here, the Appeals Chamber could not identify such a principle. This decision followed an exhaustive review of the laws of 20 jurisdictions covering three different legal traditions, including the Islamic legal tradition.[140] This approach is significant, and illustrates the willingness of the Court to undertake a comprehensive analysis of a number of legal traditions and cultures in order to assess the existence of a general principle of law.

In *Ruto and Sang*, the Appeals Chamber stated that 'reliance on national law and principles as per Article 21(1)(c) can only be sustained where they are shown to be reflective of a general principle of law derived from the major legal systems of the world'.[141] In this context, the Appeals Chamber stated that the Prosecution had manifestly failed to prove the existence of this principle as they had only pointed to the practice of Germany, Kosovo, Montenegro, Bosnia and Herzegovina, and the United States which, according to the Appeals Chamber 'is hardly reflective of a general principle of law'.[142] The Chamber did not, however, further clarify the nature of the examination of general principles that it would find acceptable.

Bohlander has undertaken research which has shown

> that while finding general sources of international law, absent a specific negotiated statute such as the Rome Statute of the ICC, involves a review of all major legal systems of the world according to Article 38 of the Statute of the International Court of Justice (ICJ), there is nonetheless a concentration of sources emanating from common and civil law systems, and more often than not the majority of them is extracted from citations in English and from a common law background.[143]

One of the reasons he proffers for this pattern is the linguistic ability of the ICC legal personnel and the language in which legal sources are available in the ICC library.[144] Therefore, cultural diversity must be respected in terms of library acquisitions, and linguistic training must be prioritised in order to ensure that Article 21(1)(c), if engaged, will allow for a full and comprehensive review of all legal traditions, and will not ignore minority cultures, if relevant.

Therefore, while the ICC has, to date, demanded comprehensive reviews of the legal systems belonging to various legal traditions and cultures when identifying general principles, it has yet to clarify the nature and scope of the required review. While there has been no example of cultural practices being identified as general principles, the ICC's provisions on general principles does provide a potential cultural portal, through which cultural considerations, can be raised before the Court.

The Statute is silent as to whether a general principle could constitute a defence, so that a 'cultural defence' could be raised. However, the issue of whether a defence can be identified by a review of general principles was addressed by the ICTY in the case of *Kordić et al.*, where The Trial Chamber stated that defences 'form part of the general principles of criminal law which the International Tribunal must take into account in deciding the cases before it'.[145]

Conclusion

Bostian states that

> judges and others involved in international war crimes prosecutions . . . should attempt to strike a balance that will recognize legitimate cultural differences – particularly when those differences may make it more difficult to uncover the truth about what occurred – but without ignoring the danger of using cultural relativism as a shield behind which to hide atrocities.[146]

This Chapter has illustrated that the ICC framework does leave room to accommodate cultural considerations and facilitates a culturally sensitive approach to all those who may come before it, either as a defendant or a victim or witness. However, it is still questionable if the Court fully represents all legal traditions equally. Much will be left up to the future practice of the Court to ensure that the provisions that encourage cultural sensitivity are used to their fullest potential in order to ensure that justice is done. In this context, there is a burden on judges to fully appreciate the nature of the Court as a socio-cultural actor and the consequent responsibilities this entails. Chapter 4 details some of the practice of the Court to date in respect of cultural sensitivity, but the following Chapter focuses on the Statute provisions concerning defences to ascertain if cultural defences can also be accommodated by the Court.

Notes

1 See Article 5 of the Rome Statute. The Court's jurisdiction over the crime of aggression is due to be triggered in December 2017. See Stefan Barriga, 'The Scope of ICC Jurisdiction over the Crime of Aggression: a Different Perspective' (*EJIL: Talk!*, 29 September 2017) www.ejiltalk.org/the-scope-of-icc-jurisdiction-over-the-crime-of-aggression-a-different-perspective accessed 2 October 2017.

2 Article 17 of the Rome Statute stets out the complementarity principle, whereby States retain primary competence over cases concerning alleged core crimes but accept that the ICC may step in if the States are unwilling or unable to undertake an investigation or prosecution.

3 Triestino Mariniello, '"One, No One and One Hundred Thousand". Reflection on the Multiple Identities of the ICC' in Triestino Maniniello (ed.), *The International Criminal Court in Search of its Purpose and Identity* (Routledge 2015), 1, 1.

4 John L Caughey, 'The Anthropologist as Expert Witness: a Murder in Maine' in Marie-Claire Foblets and Alison Dundes Renteln (eds), *Multicultural Jurisprudence* (Hart Publishing 2009), 321, 323. Similarly, Glendon states that '[l]aw is a form of cultural expression' – Mary Ann Glendon, *Comparative Legal Traditions in a Nutshell* (West Publishing Company 1982), 10.

5 Joke Kusters, 'Criminalising Romani Culture through Law' in Marie-Claire Foblets and Alison Dundes Renteln (eds), *Multicultural Jurisprudence* (Hart Publishing 2009), 199.

6 Will Kymlicka, Claes Lernestedt and Matt Matravers, 'Introduction: Criminal Law and Cultural Diversity' in Will Kymlicka, Claes Lernestedt and Matt Matravers (eds), *Criminal Law and Cultural Diversity* (Oxford University Press 2014), 1, 1.

7 Bhikhu Parekh, 'Cultural Defense and the Criminal Law' in Will Kymlicka, Claes Lernestedt and Matt Matravers (eds), *Criminal Law and Cultural Diversity* (Oxford University Press 2014), 104, 107. He comments: 'it is argued that the criminal law is concerned with the universally common evils of human life and has nothing to do with cultural biases. This response is incoherent because, as we saw, the legal system is not an embodiment of pure reason but is informed by a particular way of understanding and ordering social relations.'

8 Mark Drumbl, 'Collective Violence and Individual Punishment: The Criminality of Mass Atrocity' (2005) 99 *Northwestern University Law Review* 551, 599.

9 This problem with international criminal law has also been addressed by the International Criminal Tribunal for the former Yugoslavia, which has expressly ruled that although reliance upon national legislation is justified this is subject to the condition that 'reference should not be made to one national legal system only . . . [but] rather, international courts must draw upon the general concepts and legal institutions common to all the major legal systems of the world' – *Prosecutor v Furundžija* (IT-95-17/1-T) para 178.

10 David Chuter, *War Crimes: Confronting Atrocity in the Modern World* (Lynne Rienner Publishers 2003), 94. Other scholars, however, opine that international criminal law has created a global order of its own – see, for example, Kirsten Campbell, 'The Making of Global Legal Culture and International Criminal Law' (2013) 26 *Leiden Journal of International Law* 155.

11 See Tim Kelsall, *Culture under Cross-Examination: International Justice and the Special Court for Sierra Leone*, (Cambridge University Press 2009); Ida L Bostian, 'Cultural Relativism in International War Crimes Prosecutions: The International Criminal Tribunal for Rwanda' (2005) 12 *International Law Students Association Journal of International and Comparative Law* 1. See also analyses of cultural sensitivity of international criminal tribunals in general by Michael Bohlander, 'Language, Culture, Legal Traditions, and International Criminal Justice' (2014) 12 *Journal of International Criminal Justice* 491; Bing Bing Jia, 'Multiculturalism and the Development of the System of International Criminal Law' in Sienho Yee and Jacques-Yvan Morin (eds), *Multiculturalism and International Law: Essays in Honour of Edward McWhinney* (Martinus Nijhoff 2009); Mark Drumbl (n 8); Jessica Almqvist, 'The Impact of Cultural Diversity on International Criminal Proceedings' (2006) 4(4) *Journal of International Criminal Justice* 745; and Fabián O Raimondo, 'For Further Research on the Relationship between Cultural Diversity and International Criminal Law' (2011) 11 *International Criminal Law Review* 299.

12 Bostian (n 11), 2.

13 Patricia M Wald, 'The International Criminal Tribunal for the Former Yugoslavia Comes of Age: Some Observations on Day-to-Day Dilemmas of an International Court' (2001) 5 *Washington University Journal of Law and Policy* 87, 117.

14 Kelsall (n 11), 150–151.

15 See Robert Christensen, 'Getting to Peace by Reconciling Notions of Justice: The Importance of Considering Discrepancies between Civil and Common

Legal Systems in the Formation of the International Criminal Court' (2001–2002) 6 *UCLA Journal of International Law and Foreign Affairs* 391, 395–37.

16 In 1948, the UN General Assembly adopted a resolution, which mandated the International Law Commission to begin work on a draft states for an international criminal court. Study by the International Law Commission of the Question of an International Criminal Jurisdiction, GA Res. 216 B (III).

17 For a discussion on the Rome Conference negotiations, see Luis Moreno Ocampo, 'The Role of International Judicial Bodies in Administering the Rule of Law' (Remarks made at the Qatar Law Forum, 30 May 2009). See also Benjamin Perrin, 'An Emerging International Criminal Law Tradition: Gaps in Applicable Law and Transnational Common Law' (Institute of Comparative Law, McGill Faculty of Law, Montreal, 2007).

18 Michael P Scharf, 'Results of the Rome Conference for an International Criminal Court' (August 1998) 3(10) *The American Society of International Law Insights.* www.asil.org/insights/volume/3/issue/10/results-rome-conference-international-criminal-court, accessed 7/11/2017.

19 See, however, Picker, who states: 'Although it is a very generalised division, the legal systems of the world, are generally separated into two categories, i.e. Western and non-Western. Within the Western categories, there is a further division into common and civil law traditions, and the non-Western category includes Islamic law, Hindu law, and indigenous law', Colin B Picker, 'International Law's Mixed Heritage: A Common/Civil Law Jurisdiction' (2008) 41 *Vanderbildt Journal of Transnational Law* 1083, 1095. See also R David and J Brierly, *Major Legal Systems in the World Today* (2nd edn, The Free Press, 1978), 421; and Emilia Justyna Powell and Sara Mitchell, 'The International Court of Justice and the World's Three Legal Systems' (2007) 69(2) *The Journal of Politics* (2007) 397. It should be noted that other major legal systems identified by some scholars, is the customary law system and the mixed-law system. However, some comparative lawyers extend their classifications to include other systems, including Communist law systems – see Jacko Hussa, 'Classification of Legal Families Today – Is it Time for Memorial Hymn?' (2004) 56(1) *Revue Internationale de Droit Comparé* (2004) 11.

20 Emilia Justyna Powell and Sara Mitchell, 'The Creation and Expansion of the International Criminal Court: A Legal Explanation' (Midwest Political Science Association Conference, Chicago, Illinois, 3–6 April 2008) http://ir.uiowa.edu/polisci_pubs/3/ accessed 2 October 2017.

21 *Ibid.*

22 Nancy Amoury Combs, 'Copping a Plea to Genocide: The Plea Bargaining of International Crimes' (2002) 151(1) *University of Pennsylvania Law Review* 1, 52. See also P Kirsch and V Oosterveld, 'Negotiating an Institution for the Twenty-First Century: Multilateral Diplomacy and the International Criminal Court' (2001) 46 *McGill Law Journal* (2001) 1141, 1154.

23 Christoph Safferling, *International Criminal Procedure* (Oxford University Press 2012), 54.

24 Powell and Mitchell state: 'To reduce uncertainty about the interpretation of international law, states attempt to design international courts in a way that resembles their domestic legal systems. States can use their domestic legal systems as clues about the court's future proceedings and judgments.' Powell and Mitchell (n 20).

25 Bohlander (n 11), 495.

26 Powell and Mitchell (n 20).
27 See, however, Ahmad E Nassar, 'The International Criminal Court and the Applicability of International Jurisdiction under Islamic Law' (2003) 4(2) *Chicago Journal of International Law* 587, 595.
28 M Cherif Bassiouni, 'Sources of Islamic Law, and the Protection of Human Rights in the Islamic Criminal Justice System' in M Cherif Bassiouni (ed.), *The Islamic Criminal Justice System* (Oceana Publications 1982), 42.
29 Powell and Mitchell (n 20).
30 Mohamed Elewa Badar, 'Islamic Law (*Shari'a*) and the Jurisdiction of the International Criminal Court' (2011) 24 *Leiden Journal of International Law* 411, 413.
31 Preamble of the Rome Statute.
32 Christensen (n 15), 393.
33 Article 8 of the Rome Statute
34 See Noelle Higgins and Mohamed Elewa Badar, 'The Destruction of Cultural Property in Timbuktu: Challenging the ICC War Crime Paradigm', forthcoming *Europa Ethnica* (2017); and Mohamed Elewa Badar and Noelle Higgins, 'Discussion Interrupted: The Destruction and Protection of Cultural Property under International Law and Islamic Law – the Case of *Prosecutor v. Al Mahdi*' (2017) 17(3) *International Criminal Law Review* 486.
35 See, for example, the cases of *Prosecutor v Kordić and Čerzek*, ICTY Appeals Chamber Judgment, IT-95-14/2-A, where the Tribunal identified the destruction of places of worship as persecution as a crime against humanity because it amounted to 'an attack on the very religious identity of a people' and *Prosecutor v Krstić*, ICTY Trial Chamber Judgment, IT-98-33-T , where the Tribunal considered that the destruction of mosques constituted an attempt to erase the identity of the group and, as such, that it constituted evidence of an intent to physically destroy the group.
36 See, generally, Leigh Swigart, 'Linguistic and Cultural Diversity in International Criminal Justice: Toward Bridging the Divide' (2016) 48 *University of the Pacific Law Review* 197; and Joshua Karton, 'Lost in Translation: International Criminal Tribunals and the Legal Implications of Interpreted Testimony' (2008) 41(1) *Vanderbildt Journal of Transnational Law* (2008) 1.
37 Article 14 of the International Covenant on Civil and Political Rights. See Rules 3(B), Rule 3(C), Rule 3(D) and Rule 3(E) ICTY RPE and Rule 3(B), Rule 3(C), Rule 3(D) and Rule 3(E) ICTR RPE.
38 See Regina Rauxloh, 'Case Comment: Decision on the Defence Request Concerning Languages, Prosecutor v. Katanga', in André Klip and Steven Freeland (eds.) *Annotated Leading Cases of International Criminal Tribunals* (Intersentia 2014), 664.
39 See, for example, the ICTY Conference and Language Services Section – see Tenth Annual Report of the ICTY to the General Assembly and the Security Council of the United Nations, UN Doc A/58/297-S/2003/829, 20 August 2003, section 339. In respect of the ICTR, see First Annual Report of the ICTR to the General Assembly and the Security Council of the United Nations, UN Doc, A/51/399-S/1996/778, 24 September 1996, section 64.
40 See Nancy Schweda Nicholson, 'Interpreting at the International Criminal Court: Linguistic Issues and Challenges' (EULITA Conference Antwerp November 2009) http://eulita.eu/sites/default/files/Interpreting%20at%20the%20ICC.pdf accessed 2 October 2017.

41 Article 50(1) of the Rome Statute. This states: 'The official languages of the Court shall be Arabic, Chinese, English, French, Russian and Spanish. The judgements of the Court, as well as other decisions resolving fundamental issues before the Court, shall be published in the official languages.'
42 Article 50(2) of the Rome Statute.
43 Article 50(3) of the Rome Statute.
44 See Rule 22(1) of the Rules of Procedure and Evidence regarding defence counsel, and Article 36(3)(c) of the Rome Statute regarding judges.
45 Article 55(1)(c) of the Rome Statute states that a person. . . '[s]hall, if questioned in a language other than a language the person fully understands and speaks, have, free of any cost, the assistance of a competent interpreter and such translations as are necessary to meet the requirements of fairness'. Article 67(1)(a) includes among the rights of the accused, the right '[t]o be informed promptly and in detail of the nature, cause and content of the charge, in a language which the accused fully understands and speaks'.
46 Jonneke Koomen, 'Language Work at International Criminal Courts' (2004) 16(4) *International Feminist Journal of Politics* 581.
47 Interview by David P Briand and Leigh Swigart with Diederick Zanen, Operational Interpretation Coordinator, ICC, The Hague, Neth. 1, 28–29 (May 4, 2015), reprinted in Leigh Swigart, 'Linguistic and Cultural Diversity in International Criminal Justice: Toward Bridging the Divide' (2016) 48 *University of the Pacific Law Review* 197.
48 See generally Bostian (n 11).
49 *The Prosecutor v Akayesu, Judgment*, 2 September 1998, para 130.
50 *Ibid.*, paras 155–156.
51 *Ibid.*, para 146.
52 *Prosecutor v Rutaganda*, Case No ICTR-96-3-T, Trial Chamber, Judgment, 6 December 1999, para 23. The culturally sensitive approach to assessing the testimony of witnesses was upheld on appeal – *Prosecutor v Rutaganda*, Case No ICTR-96-3-A, Appeals Chamber, Judgment, 26 May 2003, paras 222–232.
53 *Prosecutor v Musema*, Case No ICTR-96-13-A, Trial Chamber, Judgment and Sentence, 27 January 2000, para 104.
54 Renteln comments: 'The treatment and protection of witnesses requires cultural awareness and sensitivity.' Alison Dundes Rentelm, 'Cultural Defences in International Criminal Tribunals: A Preliminary Consideration of the Issues' (2011) 18 *Southwestern Journal of International Law* 267, 276.
55 Rule 18(d) of the Rules of Procedure and Evidence of the ICC, reproduced from the Official Records of the Assembly of States Parties to the Rome Statute of the International Criminal Court, First session, New York, 3–10 September 2002 (ICC-ASP/1/3 and Corr.1), part II.A.
56 Rule 18(e) of the Rules of Procedure and Evidence of the ICC, *ibid*.
57 See Roger Derham and Nicole Derham, 'From Ad Hoc to Hybrid – The Rules and Regulations Governing Reception of Expert Evidence at the International Criminal Court' (2010) 14 *International Journal of Evidence and Proof* 25.
58 Regulations of the Court. Adopted by the judges of the Court on 26 May 2004 Fifth Plenary Session The Hague, 17– 28 May 2004 Official documents of the International Criminal Court ICC-BD/01-01-04.
59 Registry Regulation 56 expands on Court Regulation 44. Regulations of the Registry, ICC-BD/03-01-06-Rev.1

60 www.icc-cpi.int/iccdocs/PIDS/other/180815-List-of-Experts-Eng.pdf accessed 2 October 2017.

61 Regulation 44(2), Regulations of the Court (n 58).

62 Regulation 54(m), *ibid.*

63 *Prosecutor v Thomas Lubanga Dylio,* ICC-01/04-01/06-1069, Decision on the procedures to be adopted for instructing expert witnesses, 10 December 2007, para 16.

64 *Ibid.*, Section E(v).

65 Dundes Renteln (n 54), 282.

66 Articles 64(9)(a) and 69(4) of the Rome Statute.

67 Dundes Renteln (n 54), 284.

68 Article 36(3)(b) of the Rome Statute. It should be noted that a candidate for a position of judge may be qualified to be included on both lists – Article 36(5).

69 Article 39 of the Rome Statute.

70 Kelsall (n 11), 3.

71 Article 76 of the Rome Statute. See also, Rule 143, Rules of Procedure and Evidence of the ICC.

72 Article 76 of the Rome Statute.

73 Article 77 of the Rome Statute.

74 Article 78 of the Rome Statute.

75 Rule 145, Rules of Procedure and Evidence of the ICC.

76 Rule 145(2), Rules of Procedure and Evidence of the ICC.

77 Rule 145(2)(a), Rules of Procedure and Evidence of the ICC.

78 Rules 145(2)(b), Rules of Procedure and Evidence of the ICC.

79 Article 78 of the Rome Statute.

80 Rule 145(2)(a), Rules of Procedure and Evidence of the ICC.

81 Article 76 of the Rome Statute and Rule 143 of the Rules of Procedure and Evidence of the ICC.

82 William Schabas, 'Sentencing by International Tribunals: A Human Rights Approach' (1997) 7 *Duke Journal of Comparative and International Law* 461.

83 For a discussion of the approaches to international criminal sentencing by different authors, see Combs (n 22), 4.

84 See Allison Marston Danner, 'Constructing a Hierarchy of Crimes in International Criminal Law Sentencing' (2001) 87 *Virginia Law Review* 415.

85 See Robert D Sloane, 'Sentencing for the Crime of Crimes: The Evolving "Common Law" of Sentencing of the International Criminal Tribunal for Rwanda' (2007) 5 *Journal of International Criminal Justice* 713.

86 See Mirko Bagaric and John Morss, 'International Sentencing Law: In Search of a Justification and Coherent Framework' (2006) 6 International Criminal Law Review 191.

87 Combs (n 22), 7.

88 Statute of the International Criminal Tribunal for Rwanda, Article 23(1), Nov 8, 1994, SC Res 955, Annex, UN Doc S/RES/955. Statute for the International Criminal Tribunal for the Former Yugoslavia, Article 24(1), May 25, 1993, SC Res 827, UN Doc S/RES/827.

89 Combs (n 22), 11. However, see the case of *Ruggiu,* where the Chamber noted the requirement of Article 23 of the ICTR.

90 *Prosecutor v Ruggiu,* Case No ICTR-97-32-I, Judgment and Sentence (2000), para 31.

91 Fifteen States put forward a proposal allowing the ICC to impose 'one or more of the penalties provided for by the national law of the State in which the crimes was committed' – Proposal submitted by Algeria, Bahrain, Djibouti, Egypt, Iran, Iraq, Kuwait, Nigeria, Oman, Qatar, Saudi Arabia, Sudan, Syria, United Arab Emirates and Yemen on Article 75, A/CONF.183/C.1/WGP/L.11.

92 Rolf Einar Fife, 'Penalties' in Roy S Lee (ed.), *The International Criminal Court: The Making of the Rome Statute* (Kluwer Law 1999) 319, 334.

93 See, for example, Margaret de Guzman, 'Harsh Justice for International Crimes?' (2014) 39 *Yale Journal of International Law* 1, 3.

94 Combs (n 22), 27.

95 *Ibid.*, 46.

96 Article 103 of the Rome Statute.

97 See Case Matrix Network, *Commentary on the Rome Statute, Article 103*, www.casematrixnetwork.org/cmn-knowledge-hub/icc-commentary-clicc/commentary-rome-statute/commentary-rome-statute-part-10/ accessed 2 October 2017.

98 Ad Hoc Agreement between the Government of the Democratic Republic of the Congo and the International Criminal Court on Enforcement of the Sentence of the International Criminal Court imposed on Mr Germain Katanga, ICC01/04-01/07-3626-Anx-tENG, 24 November 2015. Available at www.icc-cpi.int/RelatedRecords/CR2015_24967.PDF accessed 2 October 2017.

99 Ad Hoc Agreement between the Government of the Democratic Republic of the Congo and the International Criminal Court on Enforcement of the Sentence of the International Criminal Court imposed on Mr Thomas Lubanga Dyilo, ICC-01/04-01/06-3185-Anx-tENG, 24 November 2015. Available at www.icc-cpi.int/RelatedRecords/CR2015_24966.PDF accessed 2 October 2017.

100 Article 75 of the Rome Statute. See also, Rules 94-99 ICC Rules of Procedure and Evidence of the ICC.

101 Article 76(3) of the Rome Statute.

102 Article 75 of the Rome Statute.

103 Alain Pellet, 'Applicable Law' in Antonio Cassese *et al.* (eds) *The Rome Statute of the International Criminal Court: A Commentary*, Vol II (Oxford University Press 2002), 1051, 1053. Perrin comments that one of the reasons for its unwieldiness is that it is the result of round after round of negotiation and compromise' – Perrin (n 17), 76.

104 Margaret McAuliffe de Guzman, 'Article 21: Applicable Law' in Otto Triffterer (ed.) *Commentary on the Rome Statute of the International Criminal Court* (Nomos Verlagsgesellschaft 1999), 435, 436.

105 See Picker (n 19), 1099.

106 See *ibid.*, 1095.

107 See Martti Koskenniemi, *From Apology to Utopia* (Cambridge University Press 1989).

108 Makau W Mutua, 'What is TWAIL?' (2002) American Society of International Law, Proceedings of the 94th Annual Meeting 31, 31.

109 Universal Declaration of Human Rights. Proclaimed by the United Nations General Assembly in Paris on 10 December 1948 (General Assembly resolution 217 A).

110 Text available at: www.alhewar.com/ISLAMDECL.html accessed 2 October 2017. See Salem Azzam, 'Universal Islamic Declaration of Human Rights' (1998) 2(3) *The International Journal of Human Rights* 102; and Abdul Azeez Maruf Olayemi, Abdul Majeed Hamzah Alabi and Ahmad Hidayah Buang,

'Islamic Human Rights Law: A Critical Evaluation of UIDHR & CDHRI in Context of UDHR' (2015) 1(3) *Journal of Islam, Law and Judiciary* 27.

111 See Robert Traer, 'Religious Communities in the Struggle for Human Rights', *Christian Century*, (28 September 1988) 836.

112 Cairo Declaration on Human Rights in Islam, August 5, 1990, U.N. GAOR, World Conf. on Hum. Rts., 4th Sess., Agenda Item 5, U.N. Doc. A/CONF.157/PC/62/Add.18 (1993).

113 League of Arab States, Arab Charter on Human Rights, 22 May 2004.

114 See Massimo Coccia, 'Reservations to Multilateral Treaties on Human Rights' (1985) 15 *California Western International Law Journal* 1.

115 Mohamed Elewa Badar and Noelle Higgins, 'General Principles of Law in the Early Jurisprudence of the ICC' in T Mariniello (ed.), *The International Criminal Court in Search of its Purpose and Identity* (Routledge 2015), 263.

116 Malcolm N Shaw, *International Law* (6th edn, Cambridge University Press 2008), 98; See also Frances T Freeman Jalet, 'The Quest for the General Principles of Law Recognized by Civilized Nations – A Study' (1963) 10 *UCLA Law Review* 1041.

117 Ilias Bantekas and Susan Nash, *International Criminal Law* (3rd ed, Routledge-Cavendish 2007) 4. See the statement from the *Hostages* case: 'In determining whether . . . a fundamental principle of justice is entitled to be declared a principle of international law, an examination of the municipal laws of States in the family of nations will reveal the answer. If it is found to have been accepted generally as a fundamental rule of justice by *most nations* in their municipal law its declaration as rule of international law would seem to be fully justified.' *USA v List* (Hostages Case) (1949) 8 LRTWC 34, 49 (1948) 12 *Annual Digest* 632.

118 Fabián O Raimondo, *General Principles of Law in the Decisions of International Criminal Courts and Tribunals* (Martinus Nijhoff 2008), 74.

119 Charter of the International Military Tribunal annexed to the London Agreement of 8 August 1945. See Trial of the Major War Criminals before the International Military Tribunal, Nuremberg, 14 November 1945–1 October 1946, published at Nuremberg, Germany, 1947, vol I, Official Documents, 10.

120 Charter of the International Military Tribunal for the Far East of 19 January 1946, amended 26 April 1946.

121 Agreement between the United Nations and the Government of Sierra Leone on the Establishment of the Special Court for Sierra Leone, 16 January 2002 www.sc-sl.org/LinkClick.aspx?fileticket=CLk1rMQtCHg%3d&tabid=176 accessed 2 October 2017.

122 Law on the Establishment of the Extraordinary Chambers in the Courts of Cambodia, as amended 27 October 2004 www.eccc.gov.kh/sites/default/files/legal-documents/KR_Law_as_amended_27_Oct_2004_Eng.pdf accessed 2 October 2017.

123 Agreement between the United Nations and the Lebanese Republic on the Establishment of a Special Tribunal for Lebanon, annexed to Resolution 1757 (2007) and adopted on 30 May 2007 by the Security Council of the United Nations.

124 Statute of the International Tribunal for the Prosecution of Persons Responsible for Serious Violations of International Humanitarian Law Committed in the Territory of the Former Yugoslavia since 1991 (ICTY), adopted by Security Council Resolution 827 (1993).

125 Statute of the International Criminal Tribunal for the Prosecution of Persons Responsible for Genocide and Other Serious Violations of International Humanitarian Law Committed in the Territory of Rwanda and Rwandan Citizens Responsible for Genocide and Other Such Violations Committed in the Territory of Neighbouring States, between 1 January 1994 and 31 December 1994 (ICTR), adopted by Security Council Resolution 955 (1994).

126 *Prosecutor v Kupreŝkić*, IT-95-16-T, Judgment, Trial Chamber II, 14 January 2000, para 591 (*'Kupreŝkić* Judgment').

127 See, for example the case of *Prosecutor v Erdemović*, IT-96-22-T, Sentencing Judgment, Trial Chamber, 29 November 1996, para 19, where the Trial Chamber held that 'a rigorous and restrictive approach' to this issue should be employed in line with the 'general principle of law as expressed in numerous national laws and case law.'

128 See Elewa Badar and Higgins (n 115).

129 Gerhard Hafner and Christina Binder, 'The Interpretation of Article 21(3) ICC Statute Opinion Reviewed' (2004) 9 *Austrian Review of International and European Law* 163.

130 Vasiliev states that '[g]iven that the ICC positive law is a multilayered system with a high degree of 'density' and precision of legal regulation, secondary and tertiary sources will have to be consulted only in rather exceptional circumstances. . .' Sergey Vasiliev, 'Proofing the Ban on "Witness Proofing": Did the ICC Get It Right?' (2009) 20(2) *Criminal Law Forum* 193, 212–213.

131 Pellet (n 103), 1075.

132 Gennady M Danilenko, 'The Statute of the International Criminal Court and Third States' (2000) 21 *Michigan Journal of International Law* 445, 490.

133 Antonio Cassese, *International Criminal Law* (Oxford University Press, 2003), 32.

134 Pellet (n 103), 1073–1074.

135 William Schabas, *An Introduction to the International Criminal Court* (4th edn, Cambridge University Press 2011), 209.

136 McAuliffe de Guzman (n 104), 444.

137 *Ibid.*

138 *Prosecutor v Omar Hassan Ahmad Al Bashir*, ICC-02/05-01/09-1, Decision on the Prosecutor's Application for a Warrant of Arrest against Omar Hassan Ahmad Al Bashir, Pre-Trial Chamber I, 4 March 2009, para 126.

139 *Prosecutor v Lubanga*, ICC-01/04-168, Decision Denying Leave to Appeal, Appeals Chamber, 13 July 2006, paras 13–14.

140 *Ibid.*, paras 26–32.

141 *Prosecutor v William Samoei Ruto and Joshua Arap Sang*, ICC-01/09-01/11-1001, Defence Response to the Prosecution appeal against the 'Decision on the Prosecution's Request to Amend the Updated Document Containing the Charges Pursuant to Article 61(9) of the Statute', Appeals Chamber, 30 September 2013.

142 *Ibid.*, para 11, footnote 19.

143 See generally, Bohlander (n 11).

144 *Ibid.*

145 *Prosecutor v Kordić et al.* (IT-95-14/2-T), Judgment, 26 February 2001, para 449.

146 Bostian (n 11), 39.

3 Defences at the ICC

Introduction

The Rome Statute sets out a number of defences or, 'grounds for excluding criminal responsibility',[1] in Articles 31, and also provides for the defence of mistake in Article 32 and the defence of superior orders in Article 33 but the Statute does not explicitly provide for a cultural defence. However, the provisions on defences are not very detailed and, therefore, there is some room to include cultural considerations when interpreting them. In addition, the Statute makes clear that this list of defences is not exhaustive, and therefore other defences, including some with a cultural element, could also be raised before the Court. This Chapter discusses the defences that are set out in Articles 31–33 of the ICC Statute and analyses to what extent a cultural defence can be raised, based on these provisions. It also queries if a cultural defence can be raised before the Court independent of these provisions.

After an introductory discussion on the issue of defences in international criminal law, the next section considers the defences set out in Articles 31–33 of the ICC Statute, and analyses whether a cultural defence could be included within the defences explicitly set out therein. The following section then considers other international criminal defences, not explicitly included in the Statute, and questions if such defences could have a cultural element, and if they could be raised before the Court.

Defences in international criminal law

Defences are a core aspect of domestic criminal law, and the contours and nature of various defences have garnered significant discussion and analysis. The right to raise a defence is a central component of the right to a fair trial, guaranteed in democratic societies, and thus deserves such critical analysis. However, the scenario is very different in the context of international criminal law. Indeed, defences are one of the most neglected aspects in this sphere of study,[2] with Eser describing international criminal law defences as a 'vast *terra incognita*'.[3] In addition, the practice concerning international criminal law defences has been very scarce before the *ad hoc* international criminal tribunals, and indeed, incomplete.[4]

We have already seen in Chapter 1, that the right to a fair trial is protected under international human rights law, and in a similar way to domestic law, the international law right to a fair trial includes the right to raise a defence in a court of law. Article 14(3)(d) of the International Covenant on Civil and Political Rights states that '[i]n the determination of any criminal charge against him, everyone shall be entitled . . . to be tried in his presence, and to defend himself in person or through legal assistance of his own choosing. . .'.[5] In addition, the right to raise a defence was included in the Statutes of the *ad hoc* tribunals, as well as in the Rome Statute.[6] However, the jurisprudence of these tribunals illustrates that a lot more emphasis has been placed on jurisdictional issues and elements of crimes than on defences,[7] and the limited jurisprudence of the ICC shows a similar pattern, suggesting that perhaps international criminal law defences are of more academic and theoretical than practical interest.

Therefore, despite the recognition of the right to raise a defence in international law, and the inclusion of this right in statutes of international criminal tribunals, defences to international crimes remain at the periphery of international criminal law. This neglect may be as a result of a lack of sympathy towards suspects that come before international courts. Eser has stated that there are 'certain psychological reservations toward defences. By providing perpetrators of brutal crimes against humanity . . . the defences for their offences, we have effectively lent them a hand in finding grounds for excluding punishability'.[8] However, when the ICC chose to prosecute Dominic Ongwen, who himself is a former child soldier and against whom, heinous crimes were committed, this narrative may have changed slightly, and thus reliance on defences in this case may evoke fewer 'psychological reservations'.

Another proposition forwarded for the neglect of the subject of defences in international criminal law is the nature of international tribunals. As previously noted, the ICC is a court of last resort, which is charged with dealing with 'the most serious crimes of concern to the international community as a whole'.[9] Given the limited resources of the Court to prosecute a large number of people and the significant amount of investigation and examination that precede the issuance of an arrest warrant[10] or a summons,[11] it would be hoped that the people chosen for prosecution would be those who would not be able to raise a strong and plausible defence to the charges levied against them.[12] If the position were otherwise, and numerous defendants coming before the ICC were in a position to raise a defence of alibi, insanity or duress, it would lead to a conclusion that the Office of the Prosecutor had not undertaken a thorough and definitive investigation of the alleged offences and has been remiss in choosing to prosecute these defendants.

Given the 'psychological reservations' in respect of raising defences to international crimes, the question of allowing defences based on culture is, understandably, a very controversial one. It is, therefore, no surprise that the issue of cultural defences in international criminal tribunals has received hardly any academic attention, with the exception of Dundes Renteln, who follows up her extensive analyses of cultural defences at the domestic level with an introductory discussion of such defences at international tribunals.[13] It is, therefore, the aim of this Chapter, to elucidate if, and when, a cultural defence can be raised before the ICC.

ICC Statute provisions on defences (Articles 31–33)

While the right to raise a defence was included in the texts of the statutes of the ICTY and the ICTR, the ICC Statute is the first attempt to codify defences in international criminal law. Given that this is the first instrument to attempt this codification, and the fact that it is a compromise document that aims to address common law and civil law traditions,[14] it is little wonder that it has been described as 'neither a complete, nor an entirely accurate statement of defences as they exist in international criminal law'.[15] However, Cryer *et al.* comment that '[w]hile the provisions ... leave something to be desired from a criminal law point of view, they provide a sensible structure within which to investigate defences in international criminal law'.[16]

The ICC Statute does not refer to the term 'defences', which is utilised generally in common law jurisdictions, but rather 'grounds for excluding criminal liability' in Article 31. In civil law jurisdictions, there is generally a distinction made between different types of defences, normally between justifications and excuses.[17] In general, justifications challenge whether the defendant's behaviour was wrong at all, e.g. if they were acting in self-defence. On the other hand, when raising an excuse, a defendant accepts that his conduct was wrong but he seeks to avoid the attribution of criminal responsibility, given the context in which his conduct took place, e.g. duress. It is unclear from the negotiations during the Rome Conference that there was a full appreciation of the difference between the two categories.[18] The ICC terminology therefore is neutral enough to satisfy both common and civil law traditions.

Article 31(1) of the Statute provides that a person should not be found to be criminally liable in four situations, i.e. mental incapacity, intoxication, self-defence and duress. This provision also states that this list is non-exhaustive and is '[i]n addition to other grounds for excluding criminal responsibility provided for in this Statute'. Two other provisions include situations where criminal responsibility is excluded, i.e. Article 32 refers to situations of mistake of law and mistake of fact, and Article 33 refers to situations of superior orders.

Article 31(2) is a rather intriguing provision, which states: 'The Court shall determine the applicability of the grounds for excluding criminal responsibility provided for in this Statute to the case before it.' Per Saland, one of the provision's drafters, states that this provision means that the ICC has the power to refuse to apply a defence in a particular case.[19] However, Cryer *et al.* criticise this approach because a person ought to be able to depend on a defence laid down in the Statute. They counter-propose the interpretation that the court has discretion

> to determine the factual applicability of a defence before entering into serious discussion of it at trial. In other words, the Court may require an 'air of reality' of a defence to be established before permitting detailed argument and evidence to be tendered.[20]

In addition to the situations enumerated in the Statute, Article 31(3) recognises that there are defences applicable to international crimes which it does not enumerate. This provision states:

> At trial, the Court may consider a ground for excluding criminal responsibility other than those referred to in paragraph 1 where such a ground is derived from applicable law as set forth in article 21. The procedures relating to the consideration of such a ground shall be provided for in the Rules of Procedure and Evidence.

This means that a defendant may plead a defence that is not mentioned in the Statute but is established in international law and based on the sources of law set out in Article 21, i.e. international treaties, custom and general principles of law.

Mental incapacity, disease or defect[21]

A defence based on mental incapacity, disease or defect, the so-called 'insanity defence', has rarely been raised in international trials,[22] but is an accepted defence.[23] Under Article 31(1)(a) a person shall not be criminally liable for their conduct if, at the time of that conduct, they suffered 'from a mental disease or defect that destroys that person's capacity to appreciate the unlawfulness or nature of his or her conduct, or capacity to control his or her conduct to conform to the requirements of law'. Mental incapacity destroys an accused's ability to appreciate the nature, and / or unlawfulness of their conduct or to control it so as to conform to the law. A successful plea is a complete defence to a charge before the ICC, leading to an acquittal.[24]

Cultural issues as part of the mental incapacity defence

Dundes Renteln suggests that the cultural defence could be raised before the ICC as part of the insanity defence and states that '[i]t is worth anticipating that this defense could be a new form of defense in the future'.[25] She points to the situation of terrorists who commit acts of violence and who are subsequently prosecuted. She states that 'some might claim they were acting on the basis of a divine command, otherwise known as a "deific prophesy"'.[26] She continues, stating that '[u]sing this defense, attorneys might attempt to highlight the alleged religious motivations behind the terrorist actions'.[27] Clearly, in order for such actions to be subsumed under a cultural defence, a link between such a prophesy and the defendant's culture would have to be made. It would then have to proved that the defendant did not understand the nature of unlawfulness of his actions, given that he was acting under the delusion of such a 'deific prophecy'. It should be noted in this context, that the threshold of application of Article 31(1)(a) is high, in that, in order for this defence to succeed, it must be proved that there has been a destruction, as opposed to an impairment, of ability to appreciate the nature or unlawfulness of conduct. However, according to Rule 145(2)(a)(i) of the Rules of Procedure and Evidence of the ICC, diminished mental responsibility can be regarded as a mitigating factor at the sentencing stage. It is submitted that such a claim would be very difficult to prove, particularly the link between the insanity and culture. Insanity is a medical condition, which can affect people from different cultures. If a person has a deific prophecy, which has cultural connotations, this is attributable to their mental state rather than to their culture. In such a scenario, a person's culture would be a very secondary consideration (if considered at all), rather than the mental incapacity.

Intoxication

Drugs and alcohol have frequently been given to fighters in armed conflict situations, both to fuel their violence and control their behaviour.[28] During World War II, for example, *Sonderkommandos*, prisoners who were forced to work in concentration camps and deal with gas chamber victims, were frequently given intoxicants by the Nazis.[29] Indeed, Nazi soldiers themselves reportedly used Pervitin, an early version of speed.[30] Later, in the Vietnam

War, US soldiers were given amphetamines in order to combat the tiredness caused by jungle warfare conditions.[31] Drugs and alcohol are also used in modern-day conflicts, as noted by Darcy, who states that '[i]n contemporary wars and conflicts, alcohol and drugs have often played a significant role in the commission of the physical acts amounting to genocide, crimes against humanity and war crimes'.[32] The use of alcohol and drugs in conflict was indeed highlighted by the Truth and Reconciliation Commission of Liberia, which reported that '[t]housands of children and youth were forced to take drugs as a means to control and teach them to kill, main and rape'.[33]

There have been numerous recent reports that ISIS fighters have been using an amphetamine called Captagon. This drug seems to be unknown outside of the Middle East but it is made out of easily available legal substances. It was created in the 1960s to treat hyperactivity, narcolepsy and depression but was subsequently banned in the 1980s as it was too addictive,[34] and the World Health Organisation put the drug on a list of controlled substances in 1986. It has been reported that along with ISIS fighters, other soldiers and civilians, who have been demoralised by the war, have resorted to taking the drug.[35] While the drug allows fighters to stay awake and alert during long battles, when it is taken in large doses it can numb feelings of pain and fear and make fighters believe that they have super-human strength. It is thought that the Paris attackers took Captagon pills before killing 130 people in November 2015. Masood Karimipor, the regional head of UNODC for the Middle East and North Africa, said: 'Fighters recount Captagon as making them feel powerful, fearless and invincible.' He also stated that '[i]t's chemical courage'.[36]

The inclusion of the defence of intoxication was very controversial, especially among Arab states, during the Rome Statute negotiations. However, from the above discussion on the impact of intoxicants on fighters, it can be seen that use of drugs and alcohol can negate a defendant's *mens rea*. Under the Rome Statute, criminal liability only arises as a general rule if the material elements of a crime are committed 'with intent and knowledge' and, therefore, involuntary intoxication is recognised as a ground for excluding criminal responsibility. Article 31(1)(b) states that:

> a state of intoxication that destroys that person's capacity to appreciate the unlawfulness or nature of his or her conduct, or capacity to control his or her conduct to conform to the requirements of law, unless the person has become voluntarily intoxicated under such circumstances that the person knew, or disregarded the risk, that, as a result of the intoxication, he or she was likely to engage in conduct constituting a crime within the jurisdiction of the Court.

The ICTY made the distinction between voluntary and involuntary intoxication in *Kvočka et al.*, stating that 'in contexts where violence is the norm and weapons are carried, intentionally consuming drugs or alcohol constitutes an aggravating rather than a mitigating factor'.[37] However, this was not in line with the Rome Statute, where the state of intoxication is a factor to be considered in assessing the level of a defendant's knowledge and intent.[38]

Cultural issues as part of the intoxication defence

It seems as if the taking of intoxicants has become a 'culture' among some groups in an armed conflict setting. While this may not be the traditional type of 'culture', which is the subject of this discussion, it has been reported as a systematic action among groups, such as child soldiers and ISIS fighters. It is clear from the text of the Rome Statute, that only involuntary intoxication is a valid defence. The pertinent question then becomes 'what is involuntary?' In the case of child soldiers, they are given drugs and alcohol from an early age, and are thus involuntarily intoxicated. However, what if, over time, they become dependent on, or addicted to, intoxicants and take the intoxicants themselves, once they reach the age of 18? Are they then voluntarily or involuntarily intoxicated? Could a defendant claim that the culture in which he grew up, with intoxicants as a central element, had such an impact on him, that he became compelled to continue to take them and could this, therefore, be a realistic defence for the purposes of the ICC? We do not have any guidance yet on this topic, although the child soldier 'culture' is currently being discussed in the case of *Ongwen* before the Court. However, the ICTY held in the case of *Vasiljević* rejected the claim of the defence that the accused's mental responsibility was diminished as a result of chronic alcoholism. Furthermore, the drugs culture is not a culture that is sought to be protected by international human rights norms, and it is therefore suggested that an argument based on a drugs culture would fail as a cultural defence.

Self-defence, defence of others and defence of property

Self-defence is a generally accepted defence in domestic criminal law and accepts that a person is not expected to stand by while they themselves, or another person, is being attacked. However, there are limits to the act of self-defence and any use of force in self-defence is subject to the principles of necessity, reasonableness and proportionality.[39] Self-defence is also available as a defence before the ICC, which also includes considerations of necessity, reasonableness and proportionality. Article 31(1)(c) of the Rome Statute provides for an acquittal when:

The person acts reasonably to defend himself or herself or another person or, in the case of war crimes, property which is essential for the survival of the person or another person or property which is essential for accomplishing a military mission, against an imminent and unlawful use of force in a manner proportionate to the degree of danger to the person or the other person or property protected. The fact that the person was involved in a defensive operation conducted by forces shall not in itself constitute a ground for excluding criminal responsibility under this subparagraph.[40]

The Statute's unique approach to the defence of property in the context of war crimes has been described as 'a Pandora's box that is rigorously incompatible with the law of armed conflict',[41] although the ICTY case of *Kordić* accepted that the Rome Statute's formulation on self-defence may be taken as customary international law.[42] The Rome Statute approach to defence of property has been highly criticised, and David labels the provision a violation of *jus cogens*.[43] Given the rather narrow scope of the provision concerning the defence of property, i.e. the property defended must be 'essential for the survival of the person or another person' or 'essential for accomplishing a military mission, against an imminent and unlawful use of force', Schabas notes that '[i]n practice, these terms are narrow enough that the troublesome recognition of defence of property in the Statute is unlikely to have much in the way of practical consequences'.[44] Indeed, it is true that, to date, the traditional conception of self-defence has not been raised often as a reason for excluding criminal responsibility in international courts given the nature of the crimes concerned and the roles of the people charged, and the defence of property has yet to be addressed before the ICC.[45]

Cultural issues as part of the self-defence defence

As seen above, the Rome Statute will allow the defence of self-defence, defence of another or indeed, in the context of war crime, defence of property, when the defendant acts 'reasonably' and in a manner that is 'proportionate' to the degree of danger with which he is faced. These terms are frequently used in domestic legal systems; however, these concepts may have cultural implications. What is reasonable in one jurisdiction may be unreasonable in another, depending on the cultural influences concerned.

In addition, the issue of culture may perhaps be brought up in the context of defence of property, if the property in question is cultural property. Cultural property has been damaged and destroyed throughout history, particularly during conflict situations.[46] Cultural property is defined as:

(a) movable or immovable property of great importance to the cultural heritage of every people, such as monuments of architecture, art or history, whether religious or secular; archaeological sites; groups of buildings which, as a whole, are of historical or artistic interest; works of art; manuscripts, books and other objects of artistic, historical or archaeological interest; as well as scientific collections and important collections of books or archives or of reproductions of the property defined above;

(b) buildings whose main and effective purpose is to preserve or exhibit the movable cultural property defined in sub-paragraph (a) such as museums, large libraries and depositories of archives, and refuges intended to shelter, in the event of armed conflict, the movable cultural property defined in sub-paragraph (a);

(c) centers containing a large amount of cultural property as defined in sub-paragraphs (a) and (b), to be known as 'centers containing monuments'.[47]

The requirement to protect cultural property in international law can be traced back to nineteenth century instruments such as the Lieber Code 1863,[48] the 1874 Declaration of Brussels,[49] the 1880 Oxford Code,[50] and the Hague Regulations 1899.[51] In the twentieth century, Articles 27 and 56 of the 1907 Hague Regulations of 1907[52] were adopted, also seeking to protect cultural property. Furthermore, the 1919 Commission on Responsibility identified 'wanton destruction of religious, charitable, educational, and historic buildings and monuments' as a war crime.[53] The rationale for the protection of cultural property in all of these instruments is the status of cultural objects as non-military or civilian objects and the basic international humanitarian law principle of distinction requires that civilian objects not be the subject of attack.[54] However, other international treaties take a different view on the need to protect cultural property[55] and hold that such property is of essential importance for humanity and for the survival of cultures.[56] For example, the Preamble to the Hague Convention of 1954 states that 'damage to cultural property belonging to any people whatsoever means damage to the cultural heritage of all mankind'.[57] This Convention was updated by means of two protocols,[58] strengthening the emphasis on the contribution of cultural property to humanity. Instruments on cultural property adopted by UNESCO also highlight the need to protect such property because of its importance to all of humankind.[59]

The question then arises, if a person could rely on the defence of property under the Rome Statute by forwarding the argument that they committed a war crime because they were protecting a piece of cultural property? Returning to the text of the Statute, it states that the property in question must be 'essential for the survival of the person or another person'.

Could this provision be given a broad interpretation, with the survival of a person being equated to survival of their culture? It is submitted that might be too large a leap, and would not find favour among the judges of the Court. However, in the *Al Mahdi* case, when analysing the impact of the destruction of cultural property on the people of Mali during the civil war, the Chamber focused on the status of nine of the attacked sites as UNESCO World Heritage sites and found that destruction of such sites 'appears to be of particular gravity as their destruction does not only affect the direct victims of the crimes, namely the faithful and inhabitants of Timbuktu, but also people throughout Mali and the international community'.[60] In this context the Chamber recalled evidence given by a Malian expert on cultural matters who had testified that 'destroying the mausoleums, to which the people of Timbuktu had an emotional attachment, was a war activity aimed at breaking the soul of the people of Timbuktu'.[61] Therefore, though rather a large leap, this argument could, perhaps, find some traction in future cases before the Court.

Duress or necessity

International criminal law, as with domestic law, recognises that individuals may be forced, against their will, to commit crimes. The defence of duress can be raised when the accused has succumbed to pressure due to a threat to his or her life, or to that of another. In claims of necessity, the threat to the accused is as a result of natural circumstances. In both contexts, the accused concedes that they committed a crime but claims that their actions are understandable given the circumstances prevailing at the time the crime was committed and claims that therefore they should not be criminally responsible.[62] Neither duress nor necessity are included in the statutes of the *ad hoc* tribunals. However, the defence was raised in the case of *Erdemović*. In this case, the majority of the ICTY Appeals Chamber held that duress is not available as a defence when the killing of innocent civilians is involved, but the Chamber did accept that duress may be taken into account as a mitigating factor in sentencing. The minority opinion of Judge Cassese disagreed with the majority and concluded that duress, in certain circumstances, could be a full defence to international crimes.[63] Cassese identified four conditions that must be met in order for the defence of duress to be successful. These are: (1) the act was committed under an immediate threat; (2) there were no adequate means of averting the threat; (3) the crime committed was not disproportionate to the evil threatened and (4) the situation leading to duress must not have been voluntarily brought about by the person coerced.[64] A different approach was taken by the ICC. Article 31(1)(d) of the Rome Statute provides that criminal responsibility will not arise if:

> The conduct which is alleged to constitute a crime within the jurisdiction of the Court has been caused by duress resulting from a threat of imminent death or of continuing or imminent serious bodily harm against that person or another person, and the person acts necessarily and reasonably to avoid this threat, provided that the person does not intend to cause a greater harm than the one sought to be avoided. Such a threat may either be:
>
> i   Made by other persons; or
> ii   Constituted by other circumstances beyond that person's control.

The inclusion of the defence of duress in the Rome Statute helped to clarify some uncertainty in international criminal law left in the aftermath of the *Erdemović* decision before the ICTY. There has been little practice before international criminal tribunals on the issue of duress,[65] but this defence has generated some amount of academic discussion.[66]

Cultural issues as part of the defence of duress or necessity

The case of *Ongwen*[67] currently before the ICC raises issues of duress and this will be discussed in some depth in Chapter 4. This case concerns Dominic Ongwen, who is charged with numerous offences, including war crimes and crimes against humanity. The Defence in this case has also raised the cultural context of Mr Ongwen's upbringing as a child soldier and has signalled its intention to raise duress as a defence during the trial.[68]

In addition, it is to be noted that factors which may force an individual to act in a particular way will vary from culture to culture. Kelsall, in his book on the Special Court for Sierra Leone, focuses on the beliefs of a number of cultures in the supernatural and in magic, and comments that

> [m]any Africans believe in a close relation between the visible and invisible worlds, with power in the former hinging on relations in the latter. Visible and invisible spheres are constantly interacting, with beings from one world routinely intervening on the plane of another. Many humans and indeed everyday objects are thought to possess extraordinary supernatural power with the ability to act not only proximately, but at a distance also.[69]

Thus, it is perhaps foreseeable that an argument based on necessity or duress could come before the Court, focusing on supernatural elements.

Mistake of fact or law

In addition to the primary grounds for excluding criminal liability set out in Article 31, the Rome Statute also includes mistake of fact and mistake of law as a distinct defence in Article 32. The Statute provides for mistakes of fact or law to amount to a defence where they prevent the accused from formulating the necessary *mens rea* for the crime. Article 32 states that:

1   A mistake of fact shall be a ground for excluding criminal responsibility only if it negates the mental element required by the crime.
2   A mistake of law as to whether a particular type of conduct is a crime within the jurisdiction of the Court shall not be a ground for excluding criminal responsibility. A mistake of law may, however, be a ground for excluding criminal responsibility if it negates the mental element required by such a crime, or as provided for in article 33.[70]

Schabas notes that '[m]istake of fact as a defence is not controversial, and it is a simple matter to conceive of examples where it might be invoked' but continues that the Court must assess the credibility of all such claims and it 'would be unlikely even to consider a defence of mistake of fact that did not have an air of reality to it'.[71]

Paragraph 2 enshrines the 'ignorance of the law is no excuse' principle. While many domestic legal systems do not allow for the defence of mistake of law on public policy grounds, the ICC has allowed a narrow mistake of law defence, as 'war crimes jurisprudence has tended to be more flexible, probably because international humanitarian law is considered to be quite specialized and rather technical'.[72]

Cultural issues as part of the defence of mistake

The issue of mistake came up for discussion in the case of *Lubanga* before the ICC, and this will be discussed in more depth in Chapter 4. In this case, Mr Lubanga raised the mistake of law defence submitting that he could not have known about the prohibition of enlisting children in 2002. He claimed that it had not been made known to the people of the DRC or Uganda, where Mr Lubanga was during this time, that the States had ratified the Rome Statute, which included this crime. This argument was, however, rejected by the Trial Chamber.

It has been suggested that Mr Lubanga would have been better off raising the defence of mistake of fact, rather than mistake of law, in respect of the charge of enlistment of child soldiers, given that it would have been difficult to know the age of all the children being recruited, due to a lack of documentation.[73] This lack of documentation would have a link with the culture in which the recruitment of child soldiers happened.

Superior orders

The final defence explicitly set down in the Rome Statute is that of superior orders in Article 33. This defence arises when an accused claims that they have acted on the basis of orders from a superior that they were bound to follow due to their role as a subordinate. This was rejected as an absolute defence at the Nuremberg trials,[74] and the *ad hoc* tribunals, however the Rome Statute has taken a different approach. Article 33 states that:

1   The fact that a crime within the jurisdiction of the Court has been committed pursuant to an order of a govt or of a superior, whether military or civilian, shall not relieve that person of criminal responsibility unless:

   (a) That person was under a legal obligation to obey orders of the government or the superior in question;
   (b) The person did not know that the order was unlawful; and
   (c) The order was not manifestly unlawful

2   For the purposes of this article, orders to commit genocide or crimes against humanity are manifestly unlawful.[75]

The Rome Statute thus provides that the defence of superior orders is allowed only in very limited circumstances.

Cultural issues as part of the defence of superior orders

Cultural issues in the context of a concept related to the defence of superior orders, i.e. command responsibility, were raised in the *CDF* case at the Special Court for Sierra Leone, and have been discussed in depth by Kelsall.[76] Evidence had been presented at trial concerning initiation ceremonies for child soldiers in the Kamajors militia, during which, they believed, they were rendered bullet proof through magic. At trial, the question was raised if the person responsible for these ceremonies, Kondewa, who was a type of High Priest, exerted sufficient authority over the members of the Kamajors to make him responsible for the crimes that had been committed by the Kamajors on the basis of command responsibility.[77] Therefore, there was a clear link to the culture and beliefs of the people of Sierra Leone, and it is suggested that the Court should have grappled with the question of magic and its role in the lives of those involved, and caught up, in the conflict in Sierra Leone. However, the role of magic in Sierra Leonean culture and if command responsibility could be established through the use of / belief in magical powers, was side-stepped by the Tribunal, as the Chamber concluded that the evidence that had been presented at trial had not established without a reasonable doubt that Kondewa had the material ability to prevent and / or punish the crimes that had been committed by the Kamajors.[78] Commenting on this case, Kelsall states that

> [i]n some respects, the judges were in an impossible situation here. . . If the judges accepted that Kondewa had effective control on account of belief in his mystical powers, they would have been under more pressure to take seriously the defence that belief in mystical powers also worked as a form of prevention and punishment. Crucially, they would have had to form a judgment on whether the ritual taboos were 'reasonable' preventative measures.[79]

If the Chamber had acquitted on these grounds, 'they would have risked giving credence to a belief system with which they presumably disagreed'.[80] According to Kelsall, 'this would have been an unusual departure for an international court, to say the least, and would have invited the ridicule of international observers'.[81] The failure of the Special Court for Sierra Leone to deal with the issue of command responsibility in the context of magic may be understandable, given the fear of ridicule and condemnation from Western States, however, this does not render it necessarily justifiable. Avoidance of a culture clash by not addressing relevant legal questions will not develop the law, can lead to unfairness to the defendant and delegitimise the Court. Kelsall suggests that the command responsibility question in the context of magical powers may come up again before international courts because many people in Africa, Asia and the Americas believe in magical powers and people like Kondewa may be involved in the commission of international crimes in the future.

A cultural defence as another ground for excluding criminal liability

There is no independent cultural defence in the Statute, and, given the controversial nature of cultural defence arguments in domestic law, coupled with the serious crimes prosecuted at the ICC, it is highly improbable that an independent cultural defence would be successful before the Court. As stated above, however, the Rome Statute makes clear that the list of ground for excluding criminal liability included in its text is not exhaustive. The Rome Statute allows the Court to consider other defences that are not explicitly enumerated in the Statute.[82] This approach is similar to how the ICTY dealt with defences where the Secretary General of the UN commented that even if defences were not explicit in the Statute they could nevertheless be considered, 'drawing upon general principles of law recognised by all nations'.[83] Article 31(1) of the Rome Statute provides that the list of defences in the Statute is '[i]n addition to other grounds for excluding criminal responsibility provided for in this Statute' and Article 31(3) states that '[a]t trial, the Court may consider a ground for excluding criminal responsibility other than those referred to in paragraph 1 where such a ground is derived from applicable law as set forth in article 21'.[84] Therefore, technically, there is the possibility of raising a defence based on culture, but this would have to be recognised as a general principle of law for the purposes of Article 21 of the Charter, as discussed in Chapter 2. However, as it has been previously noted, no State explicitly recognises a cultural defence as part of its legal systems, although there has been plenty of *ad hoc* practice in a variety of jurisdictions. It would be difficult to conclude, on a review of all of the legal systems of the world, that a cultural defence amounts to a general principle of law for the purposes of Article 21.

Other defences, which have not been explicitly included in the Rome Statute but which have been identified as international criminal law defences, may include a cultural element. These defences include alibi,[85] provocation,[86] consent,[87] reprisals,[88] and military necessity.[89] The most obvious of these defences to have a cultural aspect would be that of provocation, because actions or events which may provoke a reaction may vary from culture to culture. However, if it doubtful if such an argument would sway the Court to any extent.

Conclusion

This Chapter has sought to analyse the ICC Statute framework concerning defences to ascertain whether cultural considerations could be included in a defence raised before the Court. While the Statute does not explicitly allow for a standalone cultural defence to be raised, it has been illustrated that cultural considerations can be included in the defences that have been explicitly included in the Statute. In addition, the Statute allows for defences based on general principles of law to be raised, and such defences may also allow for a cultural element to be introduced before the Court. However, while the framework does leave space for cultural factors to be included in an analysis of defences, the Court is not obliged to engage with such factors. Given the Western character of international criminal justice, and the dominant legal cultures that influenced the ICC's legal framework, it is questionable whether ICC judges will take cultural claims seriously if they are raised as part of defences. Chapter 4 will now analyse to what extent the ICC has been open to cultural considerations, including cultural defences, to date.

Notes

1 This is the terminology used in Article 31 of the Rome Statute.
2 See Robert Cryer *et al.*, *An Introduction to International Criminal Law and Procedure* (3rd edn, Cambridge University Press 2014), 398. The seminal work in defences in international criminal law is Geert-Jan Alexander Knoops, *Defences in Contemporary International Criminal Law* (2nd edn Martinus Nijhoff 2008).
3 Albin Eser, 'War Crimes Trials' (1995) *Israel Yearbook on Human Rights* 201, 202.
4 See Cryer *et al.* (n 2), 398.
5 14(3)(d) of the International Covenant on Civil and Political Rights. Adopted by the United Nations General Assembly Resolution 2200A (XXI) of 16 December 1966.
6 Article 21 of the Statute of the International Criminal Tribunal for the Former Yugoslavia and Article 20 of the Statute of the International Criminal Tribunal for Rwanda both reiterate the rights of the accused as including the right to raise a defence, in line with Article 14 of the International Covenant on Civil and Political Rights.
7 See Shane Darcy, 'Defences to International Crimes', in William Schabas and Nadia Bernaz (eds), *Handbook of International Criminal Law* (Routledge 2011), 231.
8 Albin Eser, 'Defences in War Crimes Trials' in Yoram Dinstein and Mala Tabory (eds), *War Crimes in International Law* (Martinus Nijhoff 1996), 251, 251.
9 Preamble of the Rome Statute. Article 1 of the Statute states that the Court 'shall be a permanent institution and shall have the power to exercise its jurisdiction over persons for the most serious crimes of international concern, as referred to in this Statute, and shall be complementary to national criminal jurisdictions'.
10 According to Article 58 of the Rome Statute, once the Prosecutor has initiated an investigation, he may make an application to the PTC for an arrest warrant at any time thereafter. The application must contain the following: the person's name and identifying information; a specific reference to the alleged crimes and a concise statement of the facts thereof; a summary of evidence and information establishing the reasonable grounds for a warrant; and the reasons why the Prosecutor believes an arrest is necessary.
11 According to Article 58.7 of the Rome Statute, 'as an alternative to seeking a warrant of arrest, the Prosecutor may submit an application requesting that the Pre-Trial Chamber issue a summons for the person to appear. If the Pre-Trial Chamber is satisfied that there are reasonable grounds to believe that the person committed the crime alleged and that a summons is sufficient to ensure the person's appearance'. A summons shall contain the following: the person's name and identifying information; the specified date on which the person is to appear; a specific reference to the crimes which the person is alleged to have committed; and a short statement of the facts, which are alleged to constitute those crimes.
12 See Cryer *et al.* (n 2), 398.
13 Alison Dundes Renteln, 'Cultural Defenses in International Criminal Tribunals: A Preliminary Consideration of the Issues' (2011) 18 *Southwestern Journal of International Law* 267.
14 Cryer *et al.* (n 2), 398.
15 *Ibid.*, 399.
16 *Ibid.*, 400.

17 *Ibid.*, 399. See also Kai Ambos, *Treatise on International Criminal Law*: Vol I, *Foundations and General Part* (Oxford University Press 2013), 304–307; and Noam Wiener, 'Excuses, Justifications, and Duress at the International Criminal Tribunals' (2014) 26(2) *Pace International Law Review* (2014) 88.
18 See Cryer *et al.* (n 2), 399.
19 Per Saland, 'International Criminal Law Principles' in Roy SK Lee (ed.), *The International Criminal Court: The Making of the Rome Statute* (Martinus Nijhoff 1999), 189, 208–209.
20 See Cryer *et al.* (n 2), 400.
21 For an in-depth analysis of this topic, see Peter Krug, 'The Emerging Mental Incapacity Defense in International Criminal Law: Some Initial Questions of Implementation' (2000) 96 *American Journal of International Law* (2000) 317. See also Natalia Silva, 'Mental Insanity at the International Criminal Court: Proposal for a New Regulation', in Mark D White (ed.), *The Insanity Defense: Multidisciplinary Views on its History, Tends and Controversies* (Praeger 2017), 307.
22 See William Schabas, *An Introduction to the International Criminal Court* (4th edn, Cambridge University Press 2011), 240. Both Rudolf Hess and Julius Streicher raised the defence at the International Military Trial at Nuremberg.
23 The text of Article 31(1)(a) of the Rome Statute is reflective of the common law *M'Naghten* rules on insanity, but according to Schabas, the formulation in the Statute 'would also seem to be generally consistent with the approach taken in Romano-Germanic and *Sharia* systems.' – Schabas (n 22), 240.
24 *Prosecutor v Delalić et al* (Case No IT-96-21-A), Appeals Chamber, 20 February 2001, para 582.
25 Dundes Renteln (n 13), 278.
26 *Ibid.*
27 *Ibid.*
28 Dessa K Bergen-Cico, *War and Drugs: The Role of Military Conflict in the Development of Substance Abuse* (Routledge 2012).
29 See Cryer *et al.* (n 2), 402.
30 Stephen Snelders and Toine Pieters, 'Speed in the Third Reich: Metamphetamine (Pervitin) Use and a Drug History From Below' (2011) 24(1) *Social History of Medicine* 686.
31 Clinton R Sanders, 'Doper's Wonderland: Functional Drug Use by Military Personnel in Vietnam' (1973) 3(1) *Journal of Drug Issues* 65.
32 Darcy (n 7), 233.
33 Truth and Reconciliation Commission of Liberia, *Final Report of the Truth and Reconciliation Commission of Liberia (Volume I: Findings and Recommendations, 2009)*, 51.
34 See: http://metro.co.uk/2015/10/19/what-exactly-is-captagon-the-drug-of-choice-for-isis-fighters-5449606/#ixzz4kckUPgKP accessed 2 October 2017.
35 See: http://metro.co.uk/2015/10/19/what-exactly-is-captagon-the-drug-of-choice-for-isis-fighters-5449606/#ixzz4kckbWmEs accessed 2 October 2017.
36 Tom Coghlan and Sara Elizabeth Williams, 'Suicide Bombers Take Their Courage from Illegal Drugs' *The Times* (28 January 2016) www.thetimes.co.uk/article/suicide-bombers-take-their-courage-from-illegal-drugs-35krdd5wg09 accessed 3 October 2017.
37 *Prosecutor v Kvočka et al.* (IT-98-30/1/T), 2 November 2001, para 706.
38 William Schabas, *The UN International Criminal Tribunals* (Cambridge University Press 2006), 335.

39 See generally, Andrew Ashworth, *Principles of Criminal Law* (4th edn Oxford University Press 2003), 135–149.

40 Article 31(1)(c) of the Rome Statute.

41 Eric David, *Principes de droit des conflits armés* (2nd edn Bruylant 1999), 693.

42 *Prosecutor v Kordić et al* (IT-95-14/2-T), Judgment, 26 February 2001, para 451.

43 David (n 41), 693.

44 Schabas (n 22), 241.

45 Antonio Cassese, *International Criminal Law* (Oxford University Press 2003), 223–224.

46 See UNESCO, *Protecting Cultural Heritage. An Imperative for Humanity* (Report for the United Nations, 22 September 2016) www.unesco.se/wp-content/uploads/2016/09/2016-Protecting-cultural-heritage.-An-imperative. . . .pdf accessed 2 October 2017.

47 Article 1 of the Convention for the Protection of Cultural Property in the Event of Armed Conflict with Regulations for the Execution of the Convention 1954.

48 Instructions for the Government of Armies of the United States in the Field. Prepared by Francis Lieber, promulgated as General Orders No. 100 by President Lincoln, 24 April 1863. Article 34 states: 'As a general rule, the property belonging to churches, to hospitals, or other establishments of an exclusively charitable character, to establishments of education, or foundations for the promotion of knowledge, whether public schools, universities, academies of learning or observatories, museums of the fine arts, or of a scientific character such property is not to be considered public property in the sense of paragraph 31; but it may be taxed or used when the public service may require it.'

49 Project of an International Declaration concerning the Laws and Customs of War, signed at Brussels, 27 August 1874. On military authority over hostile territory. Article 8 states: 'The property of municipalities, that of institutions dedicated to religion, charity and education, the arts and sciences even when State property, shall be treated as private property. All seizure or destruction of, or wilful damage to, institutions of this character, historic monuments, works of art and science should be made the subject of legal proceedings by the competent authorities.'

50 The Laws of War on Land, Manual published by the Institute of International Law (Oxford Manual), adopted by the Institute of International Law at Oxford, 9 September 1880. Article 53 states: 'The property of municipalities, and that of institutions devoted to religion, charity, education, art and science, cannot be seized. All destruction or wilful damage to institutions of this character, historic monuments, archives, Works of art, or science, is formally forbidden, save when urgently demanded by military necessity.'

51 Convention (II) with Respect to the Laws and Customs of War on Land and its annex: Regulations concerning the Laws and Customs of War on Land. The Hague, 29 July 1899. Article 56 states: 'The property of the communes, that of religious, charitable, and educational institutions, and those of arts and science, even when State property, shall be treated as private property. All seizure of and destruction, or intentional damage done to such institutions, to historical monuments, works of art or science, is prohibited, and should be made the subject of proceedings.'

52 Convention (IV) respecting the Laws and Customs of War on Land and its annex: Regulations concerning the Laws and Customs of War on Land, The Hague, 18 October 1907, Articles 27 and 56.

53 Commission on the Responsibility of the Authors of the War and on Enforcement of Penalties, 'Report Presented to the Preliminary Peace Conference, 29 March 1919', reprinted in (1920) 14 *American Journal of International Law* 95, 115.

54 International Committee of the Red Cross Customary IHL Rule 7 states: 'The parties to the conflict must at all times distinguish between civilian objects and military objectives. Attacks may only be directed against military objectives. Attacks must not be directed against civilian objects.' Jean-Marie Henckaerts and Louise Doswald-Beck, *Customary Humanitarian Law. Volume I: Rules* (ICRC/Cambridge University Press 2005).

55 While the Roerich Pact does not set out a rationale for the protection of cultural property, the previous work of the initiator, Nicholas Roerich, in bringing States together to protect such property illustrates his belief that 'the cultural heritage of each nation is in essence a world treasure'. *See* Nicholas Roerich Museum website, www.roerich.org/roerich-pact.php accessed 2 October 2017. The Roerich Pact was signed in the White House, in the presence of President Franklin Delano Roosevelt, on 15 April 1935, by all the members of the Pan-American Union. It was later signed by other countries also.

56 See UNESCO (n 46).

57 Preamble of the Convention of 1954 for the Protection of Cultural Property in the Event of Armed Conflict, adopted at The Hague, 1954. Art. 1 of this instrument defines cultural property as 'any movable or immovable property of great importance to the cultural heritage of all people, such as monuments of architecture or history, archaeological sites, works of art, books or any building whose main and effective purpose is to contain cultural property'. However, the Convention also focused on the nature of cultural property as civilian property and provided that cultural property could only be attacked in case of 'imperative military necessity'. In 1977, Additional Protocol I to the Geneva Conventions modified this approach and provided that only military objectives should be made the object of attack. Protocol Additional to the Geneva Conventions of 12 August 1949, and relating to the Protection of Victims of International Armed Conflicts (Protocol I), 8 June 1977, Article 53; See also Protocol Additional to the Geneva Conventions of 12 August 1949, and relating to the Protection of Victims of Non-International Armed Conflicts (Protocol II), 8 June 1977, Art. 16. Both of these protocols make reference to an earlier 1954 Hague Convention. See Convention for the Protection of Cultural Property in the Event of Armed Conflict with Regulations for the Execution of the Convention, adopted at The Hague, 14 May 1954, Article 4. Note that the issue of cultural property did not feature in the Geneva Conventions of 1949.

58 First Protocol to the Convention for the Protection of Cultural Property in the Event of Armed Conflict 1954, adopted at The Hague, 14 May 1954 and Second Protocol to the Convention for the Protection of Cultural Property in the Event of Armed Conflict 1954, adopted at The Hague, 26 March 1999.

59 See UNESCO instruments on cultural property, http://portal.unesco.org/en/ev.php-URL_ID=13649&URL_DO=DO_TOPIC&URL_SECTION=-471.html accessed 2 October 2017.

60 *The Prosecutor v Al Mahdi*, Verdict and Sentence, ICC-01/12-01/15, para 80.

61 *Ibid.*

62 Beatrice Krebs, 'Justification and Excuse in Article 31(1) of the Rome Statute' (2010) 2(3) *Cambridge Journal of International and Comparative Law* 382, 398.

63 *Prosecutor v Erdemović*, Separate and Dissenting Opinion of Judge Cassese, para 50.

64 *Ibid.*, para 16.
65 See LE Chiesa, 'Duress, Demanding Heroism and Proportionality' (2008) 41 *Vanderbilt Journal of Transnational Law* 741; W Epps, 'The Soldier's Obligation to Die when Ordered to Shoot Civilians or Face Death Himself' (2003) 37 *New England Law Review* 987; and R Ehrenreich Brooks, 'Law in the Heart of Darkness: Atrocity and Duress' (2003) 43 *Virginia Journal of International Law* 861.
66 See Marcus Joyce, 'Duress: From Nuremberg to the International Criminal Court; Finding the Balance between Justification and Excuse' (2015) 28(3) *Leiden Journal of International Law* 623; Peter Rowe, 'Duress as a Defence to War Crimes after Erdemović: A Laboratory for a Permanent Court?' (1998) 1 *Yearbook of International Humanitarian Law* 210 and Wiener (n 17).
67 *Prosecutor v Ongwen* ICC-02/04-01/15.
68 See also Nadia Grant, *Duress as a Defence for Former Child Soldiers? Dominic Ongwen and the International Criminal Court* (International Crimes Database Brief 21, December 2016), 1.
69 Tim Kelsall, *Culture under Cross-Examination: International Justice and the Special Court for Sierra Leone* (Cambridge University Press 2009), 106.
70 Article 32 of the Rome Statute.
71 Schabas (n 22), 242.
72 *Ibid.*
73 Michael E Kurth, 'The *Lubanga* Case of the International Criminal Court: A Critical Analysis of the Trial Chamber's Findings on Issues of Active Use, Age, and Gravity' (2013) 5(2) *Goettingen Journal of International Law* 431, 448.
74 Article 8 of the Nuremberg Charter provides that: 'The fact that the Defendant acted pursuant to order of his Government or of a superior shall not free him from responsibility, but may be considered in mitigation of punishment if the Tribunal determines that justice so requires.'
75 Article 33 of the Rome Statute.
76 *Prosecutor v Fofana and Kondewa*, Case No. SCSL-04-14-A, Judgment (2 August 2007) and Appeals Judgment (May 28, 2008).
77 Command responsibility is provided for in Article 6(3) of the Statute of the Special Court for Sierra Leone.
78 See Kelsall (n 69), 126–128.
79 *Ibid*, 144–145.
80 *Ibid.*
81 *Ibid.*
82 Article 31(3) of the Rome Statute, referring to Article 21.
83 *Report of the Secretary-General Pursuant to Para 2 of Security Council Resolution 808 (1993)*, UN Doc S/25704, 3 May, para 58.
84 Article 31(3) of the Rome Statute.
85 Rule 79(1)(a), Rules of Procedure and Evidence of the ICC.
86 See *Prosecutor v Bagosora et al* (ICTR-98-41), Prosecution Opening Statement, 2 April 2002. See Kevin Jon Heller, 'Beyond the Reasonable Man? A Sympathetic but Critical Assessment of the Use of Subjective Standards of Reasonableness in Self-Defense and Provocation Cases' (1998) 26 *American Journal of Criminal Law* 1.
87 The absence of consent is generally considered to be an element of certain crimes. However, the claimed presence of consent may be raised as a defence. The Rome Statute provides that lack of consent is a specific element for the war crimes of pillage, enforced sterilisation, rape, sexual violence and enforced prostitution. International Criminal Court Elements of Crimes, ICC-ASP/1/3

(part II-B) (2002), Article 8(2)(b)(xvi); Article 8(2)(b)(xxii)-5; Article 8(2)(b)(xxii)-6; Article 8(2)(e)(vi)-3. It is to be noted that special attention attaches to the issue of consent in the context of sexual offences before international criminal tribunals. See W Schomburg and I Peterson, 'Genuine Consent to Sexual Violence under International Criminal Law' (2007) 101(1) *American Journal of International Law* 121.

88 See Shane Darcy, 'The Evolution of the Law of Belligerent Reprisals' (2003) 175 *Military Law Review* 184.

89 See Françoise Hampson, 'Military Necessity' in Roy Gitman and David Rieff (eds), *Crimes of War: What the Public Should Know* (WW Norton & Company 1999), 251.

4 ICC practice

Introduction

The ICC has only opened investigations in 11 situations, and all but one of these have been in African States, i.e. twice in the Central African Republic, Burundi, Côte d'Ivoire, Darfur in Sudan, the Democratic Republic of the Congo, Kenya, Libya, Mali, Uganda and Georgia.[1] The OTP is also currently undertaking preliminary examinations in eight situations, i.e. Afghanistan, Colombia, Gabon, Guinea, Iraq / the United Kingdom, Nigeria, Palestine, and Ukraine.[2] There have, so far, been 42 defendants[3] identified by the issuing of arrest warrants[4] or summonses,[5] but some people for whom arrest warrants have been issued remain at large. ICC cases to date have resulted in four convictions, i.e. *Lubanga*,[6] *Katanga*,[7] *Bemba*[8] and *Al Mahdi*.[9] While numerous cultural issues arose during these cases, including in relation to linguistic diversity, the cultural context of child soldiers, and the destruction of cultural property, there has been no discussion by the Court of the issue of cultural defences. The aim of this Chapter is to highlight some of the early practice of the Court with regard to cultural issues and analyse where cultural defences could have played a part. In particular, this Chapter includes an analysis of linguistic diversity as an aspect of cultural accommodation, the cultural context of child soldiers, and the destruction of cultural property. The first part of this discussion focuses on the question of linguistic diversity and how linguistic challenges were dealt with by the Court in the case of *Katanga*. The next section then discusses the issue of child soldiers and includes a review of the cases of *Lubanga* and *Ongwen*. The *Ongwen* case is currently ongoing before the Court and Mr Ongwen's defence team has raised a number of issues concerning defences and Mr Ongwen's position as a former child soldier, which will, no doubt, garner additional attention as the case progresses. The final section then provides an analysis of the *Al Mahdi* case, which centred on the issue of the destruction of cultural property.

This section will highlight how the Court neglected to engage fully with important cultural aspects of the case.

Linguistic diversity

As was discussed in Chapter 2, the Rome Statute and the Rules of Evidence and Procedure of the ICC provide space for cultural factors to be considered at different stages of cases, the main one being linguistic diversity. The issue of language rights of the accused and the right to an interpreter was analysed in a number of decisions in the case of *Katanga*,[10] which focused in depth on Article 67(1)(f) of the Statute. This provision provides for the right

> to have, free of any cost, the assistance of a competent interpreter and such translations as are necessary to meet the requirements of fairness, if any of the proceedings of or documents presented to the Court are not in a language which the accused fully understands and speaks.[11]

The Registry Information of Arrest and Surrender[12] states that on his arrival at the ICC detention centre, Germain Katanga spoke in French, and refused the interpretation service offered to him by Court staff.[13] Therefore, at his initial appearance before the ICC, the Presiding Judge asked Mr Katanga to confirm that he fully understood and spoke French. Katanga replied that he 'speak[s] Lingala best'.[14] The presiding judge asked if he also spoke French and he replied: 'Not really'.[15] The judge then stated that '[t]he Court is obliged, under Article 67 to have you speak the language which you fully understand. Does the Chamber understand that you do not speak and understand French?', to which Mr Katanga replied: 'I hope – I do not speak French fluently, and sometimes it is difficult for me to understand and how – difficult for me to express myself.'[16] Following on from this hearing, the Pre-Trial Chamber ordered the Registrar to provide 'any additional information concerning languages read, spoken or understood by' the Appellant.[17] The Registrar submitted its report on the appellant's language proficiency on 9 November 2007,[18] on which both the Defence[19] and Prosecution[20] made observations.

On 23 November 2007, Counsel for the Defence, pursuant to Articles 50(3) and 67(l)(a) and (f) of the Rome Statute, and in light of the fact that the Report of the Registry did not furnish sufficient evidence to establish that Germain Katanga fully spoke and understood French, requested the Pre-Trial Chamber, *inter alia*, to:

(a) take into consideration his limited ability to understand and speak French; (b) order that documents in French transmitted to him as part of the proceedings be accompanied by a translation into Lingala; (c) grant him the right to be assisted by a Lingala interpreter and translator during the proceedings; (d) order that judicial documents be transmitted to him in hard copy until he receives basic computer training and is provided with a computer and a printer; and (e) order all other necessary measures to allow him to follow and participate in his trial in Lingala, which is the language he understands, writes and speaks best.[21]

The Prosecution, on the other hand, furnished information in support of the conclusion of the Report of the Registry that Mr Katanga fully understood, read and spoke French, and that his understanding of the French language satisfied the standard set by Articles 67(l)(a) and (f) of the Statute and was sufficient for him to follow the proceedings before the Court.

The Judge assessed documents in the Registry Information of Arrest and Surrender, concerning Mr Katanga's ability in French, including a document written in French and signed by Mr Katanga in the presence of his lawyer,[22] and a *Procès Verbal d'Audition* of a hearing held before the Avocat Général of the High Military Court in the presence of Mr Katanga, which also bore his signature, and in which it is stated that Mr Katanga answered all questions in French.[23] The Defence argued that although the Registry Information of Arrest and Surrender illustrated that Mr Katanga knew, read, understood and spoke French well, his competency was inadequate to defend himself from the serious charges against him. However, after analysing relevant jurisprudence from the European Court of Human Rights,[24] the Single Judge in the Pre-Trial Chamber found that Mr Katanga's ability in French met the standards of Articles 67(l)(a) and (f) of the Statute, as he had completed his education through the medium of French and previous proceedings had been completed in French, during which Mr Katanga's level of French was found to be good. This decision was then appealed, with the Appeals Chamber reversing the original decision and making a number of key findings in relation to language rights at the ICC. The Appeals Chamber found that:

1   An accused's request for interpretation into a language other than the Court's language must be granted as long as he or she is not abusing his or her rights under article 67 of the Statute.
2   If the Chamber believes that the accused fully understands and speaks the language of the Court, the Chamber must assess, on the facts on a case-by-case basis, whether this is so.
3   An accused fully understands and speaks a language when he or she is completely fluent in the language in ordinary, non-technical conversation.[25]

The Appeals Chamber found that the Pre-Trial Chamber did not comprehensively consider the importance of, or the legislative history of, the word 'fully' in Article 67. For this reason, it held that the Pre-Trial Chamber erred in its interpretation of the standard to be applied under Article 67 (1) (a) and (f) of the Statute, a standard that the Appeals Chamber interpreted to be higher than that put forward by the Pre-Trial Chamber.[26] Commenting on the right to interpretation, the Appeals Chamber stated that '[t]he inclusion of the right to interpretation in the terms provided in article 67 as a whole indicates that this right is a *sine qua non* for the holding of a fair trial'.[27] Comparing the wording of Article 67 to provisions in statutes of other international courts and tribunals, the Appeals Chamber underlined that the word 'fully' did not appear in the other instruments, and concluded that the standard in relation to the right to interpretation at the ICC must, therefore, be higher than before other courts and tribunals,[28] and also found that this approach was in line with the legislative history of the provision.[29] The Appeals Chamber, therefore, found a request for interpretation should be granted unless it is absolutely clear that the person fully understands and speaks one of the working languages of the Court and is abusing his or her right under article 67 of the Statute. The Chamber elaborated on this, stating that

> it is not required that he or she has an understanding as if he or she were trained as a lawyer or judicial officer. If there is any doubt as to whether the person fully understands and speaks the language of the Court, the language being requested by the person should be accommodated. Ultimately, the Chamber in question is responsible for ensuring the fair trial of the accused.[30]

The Appeals Chamber thus remitted the matter to the Chamber for a new determination of the request by Mr Katanga,[31] underlining that the Appeals Chamber emphasised that the request of Mr Katanga is confined to the right to have Lingala interpretation in the courtroom.[32] As a precautionary measure to ensure Germain Katanga's right to a fair trial, the Pre-Trial Chamber had ensured that liaison interpretation into Lingala was available to Mr Katanga in all hearings that he was entitled to attend since his initial appearance on 22 October 2007.[33] The Pre-Trial Chamber heavily emphasised the delays that had impacted on the case to this point, and therefore decided not to enter into a factual determination of whether Mr Katanga fully understood French, to the standard set out by the Appeals Chamber, but held that the interpretation service that had been put in place as a precautionary measure should continue.[34] A fresh examination of the linguistic evidence would have risked depriving Katanga and his co-accused, Mathieu

Ngudjolo Chiu, of their right according to Article 61(1) ICC Statute to have the confirmation hearing held within a reasonable period after their surrender to the court. As a result, eight months after his initial appearance, when Mr Katanga explained that he could not speak French fluently, it was finally decided that the provisional facilities for interpreting into Lingala would be maintained until the end of the proceedings.

Clearly, the investigation into Mr Katanga's linguistic ability was resource heavy, and encroached on other aspects of the right to a fair trial. While the Appeals Chamber's interpretation with regard to the rights to interpretation is to be welcomed, it is unfortunate that the Pre-Trial Chamber did not accord this rights adequate importance as an aspect of the right to a fair trial in the first place.[35] A deeper understanding of the importance of language and culture would have led to the same conclusion as the Appeals Chamber concerning the importance of interpretation, and would have avoided some delays. It is important to note, however, that neither the Pre-Trial Chamber nor even the Appeals Chamber focused on the broad issue of culture or cultural diversity when discussing the issue of interpretation, but rather focused on the very narrow question of interpretation and its role in ensuring the right to a fair trial. It was viewed as a discrete issue, and divorced from the wider issue of culture. A more 'joined up' approach to culture would be welcomed, rather than Chambers dealing narrowly with different aspects of culture.

Child soldiers

The issue of child soldiers was the focus of the case of *Lubanga* and is central to the case of *Ongwen*. Mr Lubanga was charged with, and found guilty of, the war crime of enlisting and conscripting children under the age of 15 and using them to participate in hostilities, pursuant to Article 8(2)(e)(vii) of the Rome Statute, and was sentenced to a period of 14 years of imprisonment in 2012.[36] On the other hand, Mr Ongwen, whose case is still ongoing before the Court, is charged with 70 counts of war crimes and crimes against humanity, and is a former child soldier, against whom a number of crimes were also committed. Both of these cases raise questions concerning defences in the context of child soldiers, and raise some cultural issues.

Child soldiers and the Lubanga *case*

At Mr Lubanga's Confirmation of Charges hearing, the Defence raised the argument that Mr Lubanga could not have known of the prohibition on enlisting children in 2002, because neither the DRC nor Uganda (which had militarily occupied the Ituri region of the DRC) had made it known to the population that they had ratified the ICC Statute. The Defence raised issues on both the principle of legality and mistake of law with this argument. The Pre-Trial Chamber rejected this claim because it saw no reason why Mr Lubanga, who was a regional political and military leader, should not have been aware of the general prohibition against recruiting child soldiers, especially since the ratification by DRC of the ICC Statute and its entry into force in July 2002 was a matter discussed by the population of the Ituri province. In addition, the issue of the protection of children in military conflicts was specifically brought to Mr Lubanga's attention at the time.[37] Even if Mr Lubanga had been able to convince the court that he was in fact unaware of the prohibition of Article 8(2)(b)(xxvi) of the ICC Statute, referring back to the discussion of defences in the Rome Statute in Chapter 3, Article 32(2) states that '[a] mistake of law as to whether a particular type of conduct is a crime within the jurisdiction of the Court shall not be a ground for excluding criminal responsibility'.[38] The Court did not address the issue of culture in this context at all, merely rejecting the Defence's argument that Mr Lubanga was unaware of the law.

Also in the case of *Lubanga*, the Trial Chamber confirmed the Pre-Trial Chamber's finding that enlistment entails accepting and enrolling individuals who volunteer to join the armed forces while conscription implies some form of compulsion. Though the defence of consent was never explicitly raised by Lubanga's counsel, the Trial Chamber discussed the matter and concluded that children under the age of 15 are unable to give genuine and informed consent.[39] In coming to this conclusion, the Chamber relied on testimony by an expert witness who stated that children have inadequate knowledge and understanding of the consequences of their actions and lacked the capacity to determine their best interests.[40] It is suggested, however, that if the drafters of the Rome Statute had set the threshold at 18, rather than 15, for the crime of conscripting or enlisting children into armed forces, as had been advocated by some, the defence of consent may have held more sway, because many States allow for the recruitment of 17-year-olds into their armed forces,[41] and '[o] ne can hardly doubt that a 17-year old child is very well capable of making a reasoned choice when joining armed forces'.[42] Commenting on the *Lubnaga* case and the recruitment of child soldiers, Dundes Renteln states that

> [e]xpert witnesses testified in the case but it is unclear to what extent cultural arguments may have figured into the legal proceedings partly because much of the testimony was in closed sessions. It was publicly noted that Lubanga denied recruiting minors, and the defense argued that the children volunteered because they wanted to emulate their peers.[43]

A more in-depth engagement with the concepts of cultural relativism and childhood in the contexts of recruitment of child soldiers, even if the Court came to the same decision on guilt and sentence, would have illustrated an appreciation of different approaches to child soldiering in different cultures and helped with the legitimacy of the judgment. By elaborating on the cultural relativism argument, the Court could have underlined the importance of the prohibition of the recruitment of child soldiers and adherence to the legal framework.

Child soldiers and the Ongwen case

The trial of Dominic Ongwen, a former brigade commander of the Sinia Brigade of the Lord's Resistance Army (LRA), is currently ongoing at the ICC, arising from the situation in Uganda.[44] This case has brought up a number of cultural issues, and Ongwen's lawyers have already highlighted a number of justifications for his actions.

The LRA originated in Northern Uganda in the 1980s as a movement to overthrow the Ugandan government and protect the interests of the Acholi people. The LRA terrorised the populations of Northern Uganda before being driven out of Uganda by the Ugandan army. Since then, the LRA rebels have scattered to other countries, including the Democratic Republic of the Congo, the Central African Republic and South Sudan. It has been estimated that this group is responsible for over 100,000 deaths and that between 60,000 to 1000,000 children have been forcefully conscripted by it.[45] Ongwen is the first member of the LRA to come before the Court and is also the first former child soldier to appear before it. He has been characterised as a 'victim–perpetrator', having been charged by the Court with committing some of the same crimes of which he was also a victim. This is, clearly, a complex situation, and 'raises the dilemma of whether the ICC should take consideration of Ongwen's status as a victim of the crimes he is alleged to have committed himself'.[46] In particular, it raises the question of 'could the fact Ongwen was abducted as a child, brutalised to accept LRA actions and to participate in them constitute the defence of duress?'[47] The question of duress falls within the discussion of cultural defences, as Mr Ongwen was put under duress by the child soldier culture in which he was raised.

Between 1 July 2002 and an unspecified date in 2004, the LRA allegedly carried out an insurgency against the Government of Uganda and the Ugandan Armed Forces (also known as the Uganda People's Defence Force (UPDF) and local defence units (LDUs)). It was alleged that the LRA had directed attacks against the UPDF and LDUs as well as against civilian populations. The conflict was characterised by acts including murder, abduction, sexual enslavement, mutilation, and mass burnings of houses and looting of camp settlements. Numerous civilians, including children, are believed to have been abducted and forcibly 'recruited' as fighters, porters and sex slaves by the LRA to serve its members and to perpetrate acts against the Ugandan armed forces and civilian communities.

An arrest warrant for Mr Ongwen was issued under seal on 8 July 2005 but was subsequently unsealed on 13 October 2005.[48] He was transferred to the ICC detention centre on 21 January 2015 and his Initial Appearance hearing took place on 26 January 2015. His Confirmation of Charges hearing took place 21–27 January 2016, with the Decision on this hearing taking place on 26 March 2016. Mr Ongwen is accused, pursuant to Articles 25(3) (a) (direct perpetration, indirect perpetration and indirect co-perpetration), 25(3) (b) (ordering), 25(3) (d) (i) and (ii) and 28(a) (command responsibility) of the Rome Statute, for the following war crimes: attack against the civilian population; murder and attempted murder; rape; sexual slavery; torture; cruel treatment; outrages upon personal dignity; destruction of property; pillaging; the conscription and use of children under the age of 15 to participate actively in hostilities; and for the following crimes against humanity: murder and attempted murder; torture; sexual slavery; rape; enslavement; forced marriage as an inhumane act; persecution; and other inhumane acts. In all, he is charged with 70 counts of war crimes and crimes against humanity that allegedly occurred during the conflict between the LRA and government of Uganda from 2003 to 2005. The trial eventually began on 6 December 2016, and is currently ongoing, with the Prosecution presenting its case. While the Defence has yet to present its case, Mr Ongwen's lawyers have already raised a number of issues that can be considered in the context of cultural defences.[49]

At the Confirmation of Charges hearing, Ongwen's defence team attempted to get the charges dismissed, claiming, among other things, the defence of duress.[50] The Pre-Trial Chamber ruled that:

> there is no procedural rule precluding the Defence from raising duress at the stage of confirmation of charges, as also confirmed, *a contrario*, by the text of article 31(3) of the Statute. However, considering the nature and purpose of confirmation of charges proceedings, duress may only lead to the non-confirmation of charges when the evidence is so clear that it negates even the low evidentiary standard applicable. Otherwise, a trial is appropriate in order to resolve also this question.[51]

Furthermore, the judges found that there was no evidence of a threat of imminent death or continuing or imminent serious bodily harm to warrant the duress defence, stating:

Duress is not regulated in the ICC Statute in a way that would provide blanket immunity to members of criminal organisations which have brutal systems of ensuring discipline as soon as they can establish that their membership was not voluntary.[52]

In addition, the judges held that the circumstances in which Ongwen found himself were not beyond his control because it was possible to get out as 'escapes from the LRA were not rare'.[53] In addition, the Defence also focused attention early in the case on Ongwen's mental state[54] and claimed that he did not understand the charges and that he was not aware of the wrongfulness of his actions during his time in the bush,[55] but these arguments were also rejected the by Chamber.[56] While, unsuccessful at the Confirmation of Charges hearing, the Defence has made it clear that they would return to the defence of duress defence during trial, and it will be interesting to see if they will focus on culture as an element of duress in this context.

Duress in the Ongwen case

Mr Ongwen was abducted by LRA rebels when he was nine and a half,[57] while he was walking to school in Northern Uganda. He was trained to be a child soldier and forced to commit numerous atrocities. During his time in the LRA, he worked his way through the ranks and reached the position of Brigade Commander of the LRA's Sinia brigade, third in command to Kony. The rebel group was essentially a substitute family for Mr Ongwen. The LRA are known to abduct children and forcibly conscript them into their ranks. They then force them through a brutal indoctrination process and train them as child soldiers. According to accounts from children who managed to escape the LRA camps, the child soldiers are told to forget everything about their old lives. Those who attempt to escape are subjected to beatings and other punishments. Any sign of emotion can be interpreted by rebels as the children thinking about their home, and escape.[58] Ongwen wished to leave the LRA,[59] and attempted to escape on a number of occasions.[60] Grant states that:

> [t]he LRA's indoctrination process is brutal at minimum and abductees are drilled with fear ... Even in some cases, the young recruits were made to taste the blood of the dead child after such a killing or eat with bloodied hands while sitting atop a dead body.[61]

A former LRA child soldier, who was abducted at ten years of age and spent eight years with them has stated that:

It takes time. About six months, to brainwash the new abductees totally. What they do first is, when you are still new, beat you about 500 times. But if you are lucky it is only 200. Then they force you to watch terrible things. We were abducted as a group of students. One of us was brought in front of us and killed there so that we could see. Those are the things they do. They force us to do it. Then, second, anyone among you who tries to escape will be killed the same way. So, as this might be the first time you see a person being killed, this will traumatise you and make you very afraid.[62]

One of the reasons behind the violent indoctrination process is to 'break the identity of the child with his former life and usher him into the life of a soldier',[63] and to create a new cultural context for them. Abductees then must adopt a bush mentality to survive in their new life, with many soon forgetting about their previous pre-bush life.[64] The atrocities faced by abductees were recognised by the ICC in the *Lubanga* case, with the court recognising 'the environment of terror' to which child soldiers were subjected and stating that 'the oppressive environment deprived [them] freedom of choice'.[65] In the Pre-Trial Brief before Ongwen's trial, the ICC Prosecutor discussed the violence and coercion suffered by LRA abductees, but the fact that Ongwen himself suffered the same plight was not focused on.[66]

No one under the age of 18 can be prosecuted before the ICC.[67] In the context of dealing with child soldiers, this means that for those forcibly conscripted into an army and forced to commit crimes, they are criminally responsible and can be prosecuted for their acts from the day of their 18th birthday, meaning that '[i]n the space of a day, they are no longer considered victims of the war crime of enlisting and conscripting of children, but become criminals in the eyes of international law'.[68] There are currently approximately 300,000 child soldiers active in conflicts globally and 40% of armed forces (both national armies and non-state actor groups) have child soldiers in their ranks.[69]

It is clear from the reports given by former child soldiers, that they were subjected to torment and trauma and also that they were under a constant threat of violence and death. This was how the children were socialised and this is the culture in which they grew up. An important question in the context of defences in the *Ongwen* case is, whether the threat continues to apply to abductees who remained with the LRA after they turned 18?; and therefore, can a former child soldier be criminally responsible for acts he commits when he becomes an adult in the same environment?

A former commander of the LRA, Thomas Kwoyelo, has highlighted that Kony still exerted immense pressure on those who rose up the LRA ranks,[70] such as Ongwen. Kony used propaganda methods to deter commanders from escaping by instilling in them a fear of leaving.[71] He used the ICC as a threat, stating that commanders would be prosecuted if they escaped. In retaliation for the escape of a commander, the LRA have killed the escapee's entire family or community.[72] In addition, commanders were under stricter observation than lower ranks as they had more information. It is reported that Kony ordered the execution of his deputy, Vincent Otti, in 2007,[73] and he almost killed Ongwen on a number of occasions.[74] Thus, the threat and coercion that abductees felt did not cease once they turned 18 and it is submitted that abductees who remained with the LRA after their 18th birthday continue to feel duress.

Mr Ongwen spent over 25 years in the LRA ranks and, during that time, was subjected to severe violence and threats. Grant comments that:

> [t]he lasting effects of the psychological torment and mind games that child soldiers grow up with, and naturally, develop a deep belief in, results in a lack of any free will on the part of the individual. As such, it may be argued that the threat of death or serious bodily harm against Mr Ongwen was so real and great that he had no option but to follow orders to commit crimes, and thus his acts were necessary in order to protect the lives of himself and his community.[75]

In this context, it is suggested that the Chamber will need to assess the 'child soldier culture' that was created, and in which Mr Ongwen grew up, during his trial, especially if his Defence Team raise duress as a defence. Grant's comment underscores that growing up in this life broke his free will, leaving him unable to act against the wishes of the rebel leaders.

The requirement of reasonableness in Article 31 of the Rome Statute means that there must exist a set of circumstances in which the ordinary, reasonable person would have believed that they were in such danger that the threat deprived them of their ability to make the right choice. It could, perhaps, be argued that Mr Ongwen was acting reasonably in order to avoid his own certain death, by carrying out the crimes with which he is charged. However, the extreme violence and cruelty of some of Mr Ongwen's acts is clear and thus, it is questionable whether a reasonable person, in the same situation, would have acted in the same way.[76]

Article 31(1)(d) requires that 'the person does not intend to cause a greater harm than the one sought to be avoided' in order for a defence of duress to be successful. This element would be the most difficult to satisfy in the case of *Ongwen*, given the numerous heinous crimes with which he is charged, including the killing of innocent civilians. Some reports state that Mr Ongwen's acts went further than was required to merely survive and were actually aimed at him 'thriving' within the ranks of the LRA,[77] thus, it is questionable whether the proportionality element of Article 31(1)(d) could be met in this case.[78]

The destruction of cultural property

The ICC case in which the most discussion of cultural issues has occurred to date is that of *Al Mahdi*, which focused on the destruction wrought on cultural property in Timbuktu in Mali in 2012. Numerous UNESCO World Heritage sites, including mausoleums and mosques were targeted, damaged and destroyed. *Al Mahdi* was the first case before the ICC that focused on the destruction of cultural property, and indeed, the first case before an international criminal tribunal that had the destruction of cultural property as the sole charge. Thus, this case focused squarely on cultural issues, but on the destruction of culture, rather than on cultural defences. However, the case raised a number of interesting arguments about the protection of cultural property under international law, the role of the ICC in the protection of this, and, more broadly, about the culture clash at the Court.

The city of Timbuktu was renowned for its cultural property, and was known as the City of the 333 Saints. The city had numerous mausoleums, which were shrines to the saints and ancestors of the local population, and were venerated by the locals, who believed that the monuments protected them from harm. During the civil war, which was fought between a number of rebel groups, monuments were razed to rubble, manuscripts were destroyed and the culture of the city was damaged irreparably. The Office of the Prosecutor began a preliminary examination of the Situation in Mali since January 2012 on 13 July 2012, after a self-referral.[79] In deciding to proceed with the investigation in Mali, the Prosecutor stated that 'the information available does not provide a reasonable basis to believe that crimes against humanity under Article 7 have been committed in the Situation in Mali',[80] but she did reserve the right to re-evaluate this issue at a future date.[81] Therefore, the arrest warrant that was issued against Mr Al Mahdi on 18 September 2015 focused only on war crimes, i.e. the intentional directing of attacks against historic monuments and/or buildings dedicated to religion, including nine mausoleums and one mosque in Timbuktu, between about 30 June 2012 and 10 July 2012.[82] The Document containing Charges was filed by the Prosecutor on 17 December 2015,[83] containing a single charge under Article 8(2)(e)(iv) of the Statute.[84] The Confirmation of Charges hearing took place in March 2016 and the charges were confirmed on 24 March, with Mr Al Mahdi being committed to trial.[85] During this hearing, however, he informed the Court of his intention to plead guilty to the charges.[86]

The trial was held between 22 and 24 August 2016,[87] during which he made an admission of guilt. The judgment was issued on 27 September 2016, with Mr Al Mahdi being sentenced to nine years in prison.[88]

Mr Al Mahdi was a member of the Islamic fundamentalist group, Ansar Dine, and head of its morality police, the *Hisbah*, which was responsible for the destruction of numerous buildings and sites of cultural value in Mali, many of which were listed on the UNESCO World Heritage List.[89] The Pre-Trial Chamber found that the mission of the *Hisbah* was 'to prevent apparent vice and to promote virtue as well as to carry out charitable tasks'[90] and the organisation was tasked with 'the prevention of anything that can be considered as worshipping the tombs, such as building the dome over the tomb'.[91] In June 2012, the leader of Ansar Dine, Iyad Ag Ghaly, after consultation with other Islamic leaders in the region, decided to destroy the mausoleums,[92] as veneration of such sites clashed with the fundamentalist view of Islam subscribed to by Ansar Dine. Mr Al Mahdi originally recommended against destroying the mausoleums in order to maintain a good relationship between the occupying groups and the local population,[93] but subsequently carried out Ag Ghaly's wishes and wrote a sermon on the destruction of the mausoleums to be read out at Friday prayer.[94] He proclaimed that the destruction of the domes had been ordered by 'le Messager', and that the destruction was not prohibited by the religious sources which he had consulted.[95] Mr Al Mahdi had significant involvement in the destruction of the sites; in some attacks he used a pickaxe to undertake the destruction himself, while at other sites he supervised the attacks, providing tools and preparing drinks for others.[96] Video-tapes of Mr Al Mahdi participating in the attacks had been introduced into evidence by the Prosecution. In all, ten of the most important cultural sites in Timbuktu were attacked and destroyed by Mr Al Mahdi and others as part of the same common plan. These were: the Sidi Mahamoud Ben Omar Mohamed Aquit Mausoleum, the Sheikh Mohamed Mahmoud Al Arawani Mausoleum,[97] the Sheik Sidi El Mokhtar Ben Sidi Mouhammad Al Kabir Al Kounti Mausoleum,[98] the Alpha Moya Mausoleum,[99] the Sheik Mouhamad El Mikki Mausoleum,[100] the Sheik Abdoul Kassim Attouaty Mausoleum,[101] the Sheik Sidi Ahmed Ben Amar Arragadi Mausoleum,[102] the door of the Sidi Yahia Mosque,[103] the Bahaber Babadié Mausoleum and the Ahmed Fulane Mausoleum, both adjoining the Djingareyber Mosque.[104] These sites were either fully or partially destroyed by individuals using a variety of weapons, including pickaxes and iron bars. All but one site were classified as world heritage sites and protected by the UNESCO 1972 Convention on the Protection of the World Cultural and Natural Heritage.[105]

Throughout the *Al Mahdi* case, significant attention was focused on cultural issues. Both the Office of the Prosecutor and the Chamber frequently referred to the importance of cultural property to humanity throughout various stages of the case. For example, at the Confirmation of Charges hearing, the Prosecutor commented that: '[t]he destruction of such monuments constitutes the annihilation of structures that had survived the ravages of time and which stood as testimony to Timbuktu's glorious past and important place in history and to its people over generations'.[106] The Chamber took a similar approach in its Judgment, recalling the testimony of a UNESCO expert that 'the entire international community, in the belief that heritage is part of cultural life, is suffering as a result of the destruction of the protected sites'.[107] The Chamber thus concluded that the targeted sites were not simply religious buildings 'but had also a symbolic and emotional value for the inhabitants of Timbuktu' and that this was 'relevant in assessing the gravity of the crime committed'.[108]

Because Mr Al Mahdi had entered a guilty plea, the issue of defences did not arise as such. While Al Mahdi pleaded guilty and apologised for his actions prior to the trial, his Defence Team had made statements providing justifications for his actions in directing these attacks and had hinted that Al Mahdi's actions were of a political rather than a criminal nature. His lawyer, Jean-Louis Gilissen, stated that Al Mahdi

> was concerned about the common good and concerned about doing what is right, wanted to make a contribution to introducing what he was taught and what he had understood was the divine message, concerned with doing what is right, seeking the means to allow his conception of good over evil to prevail, he believed and he wanted to introduce and, if necessary, to impose purity.. [*sic.*].[109]

Gilissen went on to comment that '[w]e're talking about two visions of the world that are in contradiction'.[110] It was thus suggested that at the time of the commission of the crimes, Mr Al Mahdi believed what he was doing was correct and that he was under a divine obligation to carry out the destruction of the religious sites. This belief was based on fundamentalist Islamic principles, including *hisbah* and *ziyara*.

Hisbah[111]

The concept of *hisbah*, a cardinal Qur'anic principle,[112] is derived from the Qur'anic verse 3:104, which instructs Muslims to command good and forbid evil (al-amr bi'l-ma'ruf wa'l-nahy 'an al-munkar). Article 4 of the Universal Islamic Declaration of Human Rights (1981) defines *hisbah* as 'the right and duty of every person to defend the rights of any other person and the community in general'.[113] According to one *hadīth* (oral traditions attributed to Prophet Muhammad), Muslims are encouraged to carry out *hisbah* in accordance with their ability in at least three ways:

> Whoever among you sees an evil action, let him change it with his hand (by taking action); if he cannot, then with his tongue (by speaking out); and if he cannot, then with his heart (by hating it and feeling it is wrong), and that is the weakest of faith.[114]

While what constitutes good and evil is decided with reference to *Shari'a*, it is clear that this is a very subjective issue and that the question may be answered differently, depending on one's own views. It should be noted, however, that in enforcing *hisbah* a greater mischief than the one that is to be prevented should not be perpetrated.[115] *Hisbah* is currently utilised by a number of States, and extremist groups in the Arab World.[116]

Ziyara[117]

Ziyara can be translated as 'visitation', and the term encompasses visiting religious sites such as tombs, mausoleums and shrines. The act of *ziyara* is a controversial practice amongst Muslims, upon which there are contrasting opinions. While it is a strong tradition among Shi'ite Muslims to go on pilgrimages to visit the graves of Ali ibn Abi Talib (600–c.661) and Husayn ibn Ali (624–680), Wahhabis have consistently denounced the veneration of saints, as a manifestation of polytheism. There are early examples of tombs being destroyed, e.g. the desecration of Umayyad tombs by the early Abbasids,[118] and of Abu Hanifa's and Abu Yusuf's tombs by the Safavids[119] in the early sixteenth century. The different views on visitation stem partly from the lack of Qur'anic sources on this topic. In addition, some *hadiths* condemn, while others support, this practice, leaving significant room for interpretation. Regarding the specific issue of images and idols depicted by the Qur'an as a 'means by which people have been led astray',[120] none of its 6,236 verses actually prescribe the destruction of idols. However, verses 21:56–57 narrate, without condemning, the actual breaking of idols by Abraham in order to guide his people to the oneness of God.[121]

Islamic scholarly analysis of the correct interpretation of visitation can be traced back to Ibn Taymiyya (1263–1328), a Syrian Hanbalite jurist and theologian, who condemned the widespread practice,[122] but this view was not shared by other Hanbali scholars, such as Abd al-Ghani al-Maqdisi.[123] Ibn Taymiyya's views ultimately influenced the cleric 'Abd al-Wahhab (1703–1792), the founder of Wahhabism, a puritanical doctrine that advocated a return to the practice of the earliest generations of Islam (*salaf al-salih*). However, the Wahhabi view went further and advocated the destruction of all shrines and religious sites which were considered to encourage polytheism (*shirk*). The Wahhabis have since been involved in the destruction of numerous tombs, a practice that has unfortunately become a hallmark of recent conflicts in Syria and indeed, in Mali. Here, Ansar Dine sought to forcibly establish an Islamic State based on strict Shari'a precepts, which included, according to group's spokesman, Sanda Ould Boumama, the demolition of every mausoleum in the city of Timbuktu, considered as *haram* (forbidden) and idolatrous as they represented the local Sufi version of Islam.

However, the Trial Chamber in the *Al Mahdi* case did not examine the influence of the *hisbah* or the concept of *ziyara* on Mr Al Mahdi's actions. The Chamber considered the testimony of a number of expert witnesses on issues pertaining to culture and the value of cultural property, including a UNESCO expert and an expert on Malian culture, but did not consider any evidence on Mr Al Mahdi's motivations for his actions, and if his religious beliefs or culture impacted on his behaviour. Returning to Dundes Renteln's argument, discussed in Chapter 3, that the insanity defence could have cultural / religious elements and could be raised when individuals commit violence, 'some might claim they were acting on the basis of a divine command, otherwise known as a "deific prophesy". Using this defense, attorneys might attempt to highlight the alleged religious motivations behind the terrorist actions.'[124] In addition, membership of the *hisbah* could fall within a broadly conceived concept of self-defence of 'self', if this could be broad enough to encompass group identity. Furthermore, the defence of mistake of law could be raised given that there is a clash between the Islamic law and international criminal. However, this is more doubtful as the Statute prohibits attacks on cultural property, with Article 32(2) of the Statute stating that a 'mistake of law as to whether a particular type of conduct is a crime within the jurisdiction of the Court shall not be a ground for excluding criminal responsibility'.[125]

While it is not suggested that these defences could have, or should have, succeeded, it is proposed that the religious motivations and cultural context of the crimes committed deserved additional attention from the Chamber. The Chamber should have engaged with the concepts of *hisbah* and *ziyara* in more depth and analysed the impact of these precepts of Islamic law on Mr Al Mahdi. While the Chamber's lack of engagement with the impact of religious / cultural factors on Mr Al Mahdi's actions may be justified as he had already entered a guilty plea, and indeed, issued an apology for his actions,[126] it is submitted that a discussion of relevant Islamic law – even if the Court had rejected the Wahhabi interpretation – could have placated a number of States who view the Court as a Western imperialist institution. By ignoring this religious / cultural component of the destruction of cultural property, the Court missed an opportunity to illustrate its respect for all legal traditions.

Cultural considerations in the Al Mahdi *Reparations Decision*

The devastating destruction caused to the cultural property of Timbuktu as a result of Mr Al Mahdi's and other's actions is without doubt. Thankfully, UNESCO, supported by other stakeholders, has now rebuilt or restored the destroyed and damaged sites.[127] This goes some way to repair the emotional damage caused to the local population in Mali, as does the ICC Reparations Order, issued on 17 August 2017. The Chamber held that Mr Al Mahdi was liable for €2.7 million in total for the damage caused by the attack of nine mosques and the Sidi Yahia Mosque door; the economic loss caused to the individuals whose livelihoods depended upon the tourism and maintenance of these 'Protected Buildings' and to the community of Timbuktu as a whole; and the moral harm caused by the attacks. In total, UNESCO spent over €2.53 million in rebuilding all of the mausoleums and rehabilitating the mosques and libraries, which had been destroyed in Timbuktu,[128] and the Chamber calculated that Mr Al Mahdi's liability was €97,000.[129] In respect of consequential economic loss, the Chamber assessed Mr Al Mahdi to be responsible for €2.12 million. Finally, while highlighting the inherent difficulty in allocating a monetary measure for moral harm, the Court set his liability in this category at €483,000.[130] Mr Al Mahdi's total liability, therefore, was assessed to be €2.7 million.[131] The Chamber, however, recognised that, at present, Mr Al Mahdi was not capable of paying the reparations.[132] Throughout the Reparations Decision, the Chamber focused on cultural issues and the impact of the destruction of the cultural property on the culture and people on Timbuktu. According to Balta and Banteka, the decision 'demonstrates respect for the culture of the victims, and by providing reparations, the Court created precedent for protecting the spiritual and religious connection between the victimized communities and protected buildings'.[133]

The Chamber received 139 reparations applications, 137 from individuals and 2 from organisations. The Legal Representative of Victims (LRV) represented all of the applications and sought both individual reparation measures, aimed at monetary compensation for the harm suffered by the victims, as well as collective reparation measures for the upkeep, restoration and rehabilitation of the Protected Buildings.[134] As stated above, the Chamber held that reparations must be awarded for three different kinds of harms, i.e. (i) Damage to the Protected Buildings: collective reparations through rehabilitation of the sites of the Protected Buildings; (ii) Consequential economic loss: individual reparations for those whose livelihoods exclusively depended upon the Protected Buildings and collective reparations for the community of Timbuktu as a whole – these reparations are to be implemented through compensation to address the individual financial losses suffered and rehabilitation to address the economic harm caused to the community of Timbuktu; and (iii) Moral harm: individual reparations for those whose ancestors' burial sites were damaged in the attack and collective reparations for the community of Timbuktu as a whole.[135] The Chamber required that '[t]o every extent possible, these reparations must be implemented in a gender and culturally sensitive manner'.[136]

As part of the Reparations Order, the Chamber agreed with the LRV's request to award nominal damages to the Malian State for the harm suffered,[137] which had emanated from a consultation with Malian authorities, and awarded the State €1 as a symbolic gesture,[138] illustrating the damage done to the State through the destruction of part of its culture. The Chamber also awarded a symbolic €1 to the international community, which it felt was best represented by UNESCO, given the focus of the case on cultural property,[139] and the contribution of the cultural property in Mali to humanity as a whole.

Moral harm

As mentioned above, one of the categories of harm which entitled victims to reparations was moral harm. During the Sentencing hearing, the Chamber held that Mr Al Mahdi had caused moral harm,[140] and every victim claimed some sort of moral harm as a result of the attack on the buildings in Timbuktu during the reparations process. In the Reparations Order, the Chamber held that victims had established two forms of moral harm to the requisite standard: '(i) mental pain and anguish, including losses of childhood, opportunities and relationships among those who fled Timbuktu because the Protected Buildings were attacked and (ii) disruption of culture.'[141] With regard to disruption of culture, the Chamber referred, in a footnote, to the fact that forms of moral harm related to the disruption of culture were recognised in international human rights law jurisprudence, and referenced the cases of *Plan de Sánchez Massacre v Guatemala*[142] and *Yakye Axa Indigenous Community v Paraguay*,[143] which came before the Inter-American Court of Human Rights.[144] When addressing the harm emanating from the disruption of culture, the Chamber highlighted a number of submissions by witnesses.[145] These focused on how the destruction of the cultural property affected them emotionally, and the impact it had on their life, including on their relationship with their religion. Many victims highlighted the fact that the destroyed buildings were thought of as protecting the local community from outside harm and that their destruction 'shattered the community's collective faith that they were protected'.[146] The impact of the destruction can be seen in a number of statements from victims, including:

I have never suffered so deeply in my life [. . .] Mentally, I was devastated. I felt humiliated by the destruction. I am still suffering [. . .] I am still affected mentally.[147]

I lost everything with the destruction – my childhood, my belief and my attachment.[148]

I cried a lot on the day of the destruction. My family, my friend and all the people of Timbuktu suffered. We will never forget. The Saints of Timbuktu are the descendants of Allah. When we used to ask for their blessings, they would be given. When the mausoleums were destroyed, we were shattered as well. The pain is still there today. The city has changed. Timbuktu is no longer what it was; even if the saints protect us still, it's not the same as before. We lost everything; today we have nothing.[149]

Section III of the Reparations Decision is dedicated to the importance of international cultural heritage, because the Chamber considered it necessary 'to address the importance of cultural heritage, given that it is an essential component of the charges Mr Al Mahdi is convicted of'.[150] Recalling the testimony of one of the expert witnesses, the Chamber stated that 'cultural heritage plays a central role in the way communities define themselves and bond together, and how they identify with their past and contemplate their future'.[151] It is clear that throughout the Reparations Decision, the Court underlined the importance of culture and illustrated the negative impacts of the loss of culture on victims. However, Mr Al Mahdi's cultural / religious motivations were given a lot less consideration.

Conclusion

The ICC is still young, and to date, there has not been a huge amount of practice with regard to defences, and even less so with regard to cultural defences. Indeed, as stated in Chapter 3, defences tend to get very little attention in international criminal trials, and, because cultural defences are such a controversial and divisive issue, they receive even less, if any, attention. However, early practice by the ICC has shown a willingness to be culturally sensitive to a number of issues and some of its decisions have highlighted the importance of culture. The ICC institutional framework, as analysed in Chapter 2, does leave room to accommodate cultural considerations at various stages of cases, and the Court has illustrated cultural sensitivity in some of its decisions, including in relation to linguistic diversity, as seen in the discussion of the *Katanga* decision above. The Court has recognised and underscored the importance of culture in the context of the destruction of cultural property. However, this discussion in the case of *Al Mahdi*, while emphasising the importance of cultural property to a significant extent, and the devastating impact the destruction of such property has on local populations and the international community, did not engage fully with the broader issue of the right to culture or how the right to culture may impact on the Court's decisions. The Court took a somewhat *ad hoc* approach when considering cultural issues. While the analysis of the impact of the destruction of culture is important, there was a lot lacking from the Chamber's analysis in respect of the motivations for Mr Al Mahdi's actions. As stated above, while Mr Al Mahdi's guilty plea led to a truncated analysis of the case, and his apology in respect of his actions negated previous statements of his lawyers concerning a culture clash within the Court, it is disappointing that the Court did not fully engage with the Islamic concepts of *hisbah* and *ziyara*, to illustrate that it is an institution that is open to all legal cultures. It seems that the discussion of culture was focused only on the cultural rights of the victims. That is not to say that the emphasis on the importance of culture in the case, including in the Reparations Decision, was incorrect, rather that it was one-sided and incomplete.

The *Ongwen* case raises a number of issues concerning culture and the Defence has already signalled its intention of focusing more on the context of Mr Ongwen's upbringing as a child soldier and the impact that this should have on his liability. Given his status as a victim–perpetrator, it is expected that there will be significant emphasis on the culture of child solider. The Defence may not, however, take a direct cultural defence route, but rather focus on the cultural context of his actions. How the Court reacts to such arguments will be of great interest.

Notes

1 ICC, 'Situations under Investigations'. Available at: www.icc-cpi.int/pages/situations. aspx.
2 ICC, 'Preliminary Examinations'. Available at: www.icc-cpi.int/Pages/Preliminary-Examinations.aspx.
3 ICC, 'Cases'. Available at: www.icc-cpi.int/Pages/defendants-wip.aspx#Defa ult=%7B%22k%22%3A%22%22%7D#c6cbd0da-cc12-4701-a455-cb691df92 bfd=%7B%22k%22%3A%22%22%7D accessed 2 October 2017.
4 Article 58(1) of the Rome Statute.
5 Article 58(7) of the Rome Statute.
6 *Prosecutor v Thomas Lubanga Dyilo*, Judgment, ICC-01/04-01/06-2842, 04 April 2012.
7 *Prosecutor v Germain Katanga*, Judgment, ICC-01/04-01/07-3436-tENG, 07 March 2014.
8 *Prosecutor v Jean Pierre Bemba Gombo*, Judgment, ICC-01/05-01/08, 21 March 2016.

9 *Prosecutor v Ahmad Al Faqi Al Mahdi*, Judgment, ICC-01/12-01/15, 27 September 2016.

10 See *Prosecutor v Katanga*, ICC-01/04-01/07, Decision on the Defence Request Concerning Languages, 21 December 2007; Judgment on the appeal of Mr Germain Katanga against the decision of Pre-Trial Chamber I entitled 'Decision on the Defence Request Concerning Languages', 27 May 2008 and Decision Implementing the Appeal Chamber Judgment concerning Languages, 2 June 2008. See Regina Rauxloh, 'Case Comment: Decision on the Defence Request Concerning Languages, Prosecutor v. Katanga' in André Klip and Steven Freeland (eds), *Annotated Leading Cases of International Criminal Tribunals* (Intersentia 2014), 664.

11 Article 67(1)(f) of the Rome Statute.

12 8ICC-01/04-01/07-40-Conf-Anx.6.

13 CC-01 /04-01 /07-40-Conf-Anx.7.

14 ICC-01/04-0 1/07-T-5-ENG[22Oct2007Edited], page 3, line 8.

15 First Appearance Hearing – Open Session, Transcript ICC-0 1-04-0 1 -07-T-5-Lng, Monday, 22 October – 2007, page 3, line 11.

16 First Appearance Hearing – Open Session, Transcript ICC-0 1-04-0 1 -07-T-5-Lng, Monday, 22 October 2007, page 3, lines 16–21.

17 Order for a Report of Additional Information on the Detention and Surrender of the Detainee Germain Katanga, ICC-0 1/04-0 1/07-45, p. 3.

18 Report of the Registry on the Additional Information Concerning the Languages Spoken, Written and Understood by Germain Katanga, ICC-01/04-01/07-62-tENG.

19 Observations of the Defence of Germain Katanga on the 'Report of the Registry on the Additional Information Concerning the Languages Spoken, Written and Understood by Germain Katanga', ICC-01/04-01,'07-78-tKNG.

20 Prosecution's Observations on the 'Rapport du Greffe relatif aux renseignements supplémentaires concernant les langues parlées, écrites et comprises par Germain Katanga', ICC-01/04-01/07-81.

21 See *Prosecutor v. Katanga*, ICC-01/04-01/07, Decision on the Defence Request Concerning Languages, 21 December 2007.

22 ICC-01/04/01/07-40-Conf-Anx3.3.

23 ICC-01/04/01/07-40-Anx3.5.

24 *Hermi v Italy*, no. 18114/02, ECtHR (Fourth Section), Judgment (Merits and Just Satisfaction) of 28.06.2005 and *Brozieck v Italy*, 1989 12 EHRR 371.

25 See *Prosecutor v Katanga*, ICC-01/04-01/07, Judgment on the appeal of Mr Germain Katanga against the decision of Pre-Trial Chamber I entitled 'Decision on the Defence Request Concerning Languages', 27 May 2008, para 3.

26 *Ibid.*, 37.

27 *Ibid.*, para 41.

28 *Ibid.*, para 49.

29 *Ibid.*, para 51.

30 *Ibid.*, para 61.

31 *Ibid.*, para 66.

32 *Ibid.*, paras 19 and 66.

33 *Prosecutor v Katanga*, ICC-01/04-01/07, Decision Implementing the Appeal Chamber Judgment concerning Languages, 2 June 2008, para 14.

34 *Ibid.*, para 16.

35 See Rauxloh (n 10).

36 See ICC, 'Lubanga Case'. Available at: www.icc-cpi.int/drc/lubanga accessed 2 October 2017.

37 *Prosecutor v Lubanga*, Decision on Confirmation of Charges, ICC 01/04-01/0629, January 2007, paras 306, 312–314.

38 Article 32(2) of the Rome Statute.

39 *Prosecutor v Thomas Lubanga Dyilo*, Judgment, ICC-01/04-01/06, 14 March 2012, para 617.

40 See E Schauer and T Elbert, 'The Psychological Impact of Child Soldiering' in E Martz (ed.), *Trauma Rehabilitation After War and Conflict* (Springer 2010), 311.

41 See A Sheppard, 'Child Soldiers: Is the Optional Protocol Evidence of an Emerging "Straight 18" Consensus?' (2000) 8(1) *International Journal of Children's Rights* 37, 48.

42 Michael E Kurth, 'The *Lubanga* Case of the International Criminal Court: A Critical Analysis of the Trial Chamber's Findings on Issues of Active Use, Age, and Gravity' (2013) 5(2) *Goettingen Journal of International Law* 431, 437.

43 Alison Dundes Rentelm, 'Cultural Defenses in International Criminal Tribunals: A Preliminary Consideration of the Issues' (2011) 18 *Southwestern Journal of International Law* 267, 281.

44 Uganda signed the Rome Statute on 17 March 1999 and ratified it on 14 June 2002. On 16 December 2003, the Government of Uganda referred the situation concerning northern Uganda to the Office of the Prosecutor and on 29 July 2004 the Prosecutor determined a reasonable basis to open an investigation into the situation.

45 See War Child, 'The Lord's Resistance Army Profile', www.warchild.org.uk/issues/the-lords-resostance-army accessed 2 October 2017; United Nations Security Council. *Report of the Secretary-General on the Activities of United Nations Regional Office for Central Africa and on the Lord's Resistance Army-affected Areas*, S/2013/297, May 2013, para 68. See also LRA Crisis Tracker, *Update: The State of the LRA in 2015*, September 2015.

46 Nadia Grant, *Duress as a Defence for Former Child Soldiers? Dominic Ongwen and the International Criminal Court* (International Crimes Database Brief 21, December 2016), 1.

47 *Ibid.*

48 On 6 May 2005 the Prosecutor submitted the request for the warrants of arrest for Joseph Kony, Vincent Otti, Raska Lukwiya, Okot Odhiambo and Dominic Ongwen, which was subsequently amended and supplemented on 13 May 2005 and additionally on 18 May 2005.

49 See Further Redacted Version of 'Defence Brief for the Confirmation of Charges Hearing', filed on 18 January 2016, ICC-02/04-01/15, 3 March 2016 and Transcript of the Confirmation of Changer Hearing, ICC-02/04-01/15-T-22-ENG ET WT 25-01-2016 1/72 SZ PT.

50 See *Prosecutor v Ongwen*, Decision on the confirmation of charges against Dominic Ongwen, ICC-02/04-01/15, 23 March 2016, para 151. See also Further Redacted Version of 'Defence Brief for the Confirmation of Charges Hearing', filed on 18 January 2016, ICC-02/04-01/15, 3 March 2016 paras 50–57, and Transcript of the Confirmation of Changer Hearing, ICC-02/04-01/15-T-22-ENG ET WT 25-01-2016 1/72 SZ PT, pp. 48–49.

51 See *Prosecutor v Ongwen*, Decision on the confirmation of charges against Dominic Ongwen, ICC-02/04-01/15, 23 March 2016, para 151.

52 *Ibid.*, para 153.

53 *Ibid.*, 154.

54 See Decision on the Defence Request to Order a Medical Examination of Dominic Ongwen, ICC-02/04-01/15, 16 December 2016.

55 See Defence Request for Leave to Appeal the Oral Decision of 6 December 2016 on Mr Ongwen's Understanding of the Nature of the Charges ICC-02/04-01/15-632, 12 December 2016.

56 ICC-02/04-01/15-T-26-ENG, page 17, line 23 to page 20, line 4, Defence Request for Leave to Appeal the Oral Decision of 6 December 2016 on Mr Ongwen's Understanding of the Nature of the Charges, ICC-02/04-01/15-632, and Decision on Defence Request for Leave to Appeal the Decision on Mr Ongwen's Understanding of the Nature of the Charges, 3 January 2017.

57 ICC Pre-Trial Chamber II, *Situation in Uganda, In the Case of the Prosecutor v Dominic Ongwen*, Case No. ICC-02/04-01/15, *Transcript of the Confirmation of Charges Hearing*, 25 January 2016, p. 41.

58 See Erin K Baines, 'Complex Political Perpetrators: Reflections on Dominic Ongwen' (2009) 47(2) *The Journal of Modern African Studies* 170.

59 Mark A Drumbl, 'A Former Child Soldier Prosecuted at the International Criminal Court' (*Oxford University Press Blog*, 26 September 2016) https://blog.oup.com/2016/09/child-soldier-prosecuted-icc-law accessed 3 October 2017.

60 Stephanie Nolen and Eric Baines, 'The Making of a Monster' *The Globe and Mail* (25 October 2008) https://beta.theglobeandmail.com/news/world/the-making-of-a-monster/article20389116/?ref=http://www.theglobeandmail.com& accessed 2 October 2017.

61 Grant (n 46), 7–8. See Human Rights Watch, *Coercion and Intimidation of Child Soldiers to Participate in Violence* (Human Rights Watch Report, 16 April 2008) www.hrw.org/news/2008/04/16/coercion-and-intimidation-child-soldiers-participate-violence accessed 3 October 2017; and Nienke Grossman, 'Rehabilitation or Revenge: Prosecuting Child Soldiers for Human Rights Violations' (2007) 38 *Georgetown Journal of International Law* 323, 328.

62 Ariadne Asimakopoulos, 'Justice and Accountability: Complex Political Perpetrators. Abducted as Children by the LRA in Northern Uganda' (Masters Thesis, Utrecht University 2010), 31.

63 Justice and Reconciliation Project, *Complicating Victims and Perpetrators in Uganda: On Dominic Ongwen* (Field Note 7, July 2008), 9.

64 Baines (n 58), 170.

65 ICC, Office of the Prosecutor, *Situation in the Democratic Republic of Congo, Prosecutor v Thomas Lubanga Duilo, Case No. ICC-01/04-01/06, Opening Statement, 26 January 2009.*

66 ICC Trial Chamber IX, *Situation in Uganda, In the Case of the Prosecutor v Dominic Ongwen,* Case No ICC-02/04-02/15, Prosecutor's Pre-Trial Brief, 6 September 2016.

67 Article 26 of the Rome Statute.

68 Grant (n 46), 3–4.

69 Eben Kaplan, *Child Soldiers around the World* (Council on Foreign Relations, 2 December 2005).

70 Asimakopoulos (n 62), 49.

71 Grant (n 46), 10.

72 Asimakopoulos (n 62), 38.

73 Emma Mutaizibwa, *LRA Under Pressure to Back Peace Plan* (Institute for War and Peace Reporting, 20 December 2007).
74 Drumbl (n 59).
75 Grant (n 46), 13.
76 *Ibid.*, 15.
77 Mark Drumbl, 'The Ongwen Trial at the ICC: Tough Questions on Child Soldiers' (*Open Democracy*, 14 April 2015).
78 Grant (n 46), 17.
79 See letter of referral from the Malian Minister for Justice to the Prosecutor, 13 July 2013. Available at: www.icc-cpi.int/NR/rdonlyres/A245A47F-BFD1-45B6-891C-3BCB5B173F57/0/ReferralLetterMali130712.pdf accessed 2 October 2017.
80 Office of the Prosecutor, Situation in Mali (Art. 53(1) Report, 16 January 2013, para 128.
81 See Noelle Higgins and Mohamed Elewa Badar, 'The Destruction of Cultural Property in Timbuktu: Challenging the ICC War Crime Paradigm', forthcoming *Europa Ethnica*; and William Schabas, 'Al Mahdi Has Been Convicted of a Crime He Did Not Commit' (2017) 49 *Case Western Reserve Journal of International Law* 75.
82 Arrest Warrant, Al Faqi Al Mahdi, ICC-01/12-01/15-1-Red, Pre-Trial Chamber I, 18 September 2015.
83 ICC-01/12-01/15-62, ICC-01/12-01/15-63 and –AnxA (Arabic translation); ICC-01/12-01/15-70 and –AnxA-Corr (English translation).
84 Chef d'accusation retenu par l'Accusation contre Ahmad AL FAQI AL MAHDI, 17 December 2015, ICC-01/12-01/15-62.
85 Decision on the confirmation of charges against Ahmad Al Faqi Al Mahdi, ICC-01/12-01/15, 24 March 2016.
86 See 'Statement of the Prosecutor of the International Criminal Court', Fatou Bensouda, following admission of guilt by the accused in Mali war crime case: 'An important step for the victims, and another first for the ICC', 24 March 2016, www.icc-cpi.int/Pages/item.aspx?name=160324-otp-stat-al-Mahdi accessed 2 October 2017.
87 ICC-01/12-01/15-T-4-Red-ENG,ICC-01/12-01/15-T-5-Red-ENG,ICC-01/12-01/15-T-6-ENG.
88 *The Prosecutor v Al Mahdi*, Verdict and Sentence, ICC-01/12-01/15-171, 27 September 2016.
89 UNESCO's World Heritage Convention Nomination Documentation. See: http://whc.unesco.org/en/nominations/ accessed 2 October 2017.
90 *Prosecutor v Ahmad Al Faqi Al Mahdi*, 24 March 2016, ICC, Pre-Trial Chamber I, Decision on the confirmation of charges against Ahmad Al Faqi Al Mahdi, ICC-01/12-01/15, para 46.
91 *Ibid.*, para 47.
92 Agreement, ICC-01/12-01/15-78-Anx1-tENG-Red, para 38.
93 *Ibid.*, para 37.
94 *Ibid.*, para 44.
95 *Ibid.*
96 *Ibid.*, para 51.
97 *Ibid.*, paras 64-65.
98 *Ibid.*, paras 66–72.
99 *Ibid.*, paras 73–78.

100 *Ibid.*, paras 85–86.
101 *Ibid.*, paras 87–88.
102 *Ibid.*, paras 82–84.
103 *Ibid.*, paras 89–95.
104 *Ibid.*, paras 96–103.
105 *Ibid.*, para 33.
106 Statement of the Prosecutor of the International Criminal Court, Fatou Bensouda, at the opening of the confirmation of charges hearing in the case against Mr Ahmad Al-Faqi Al Mahdi, 1 March 2016.
107 *Ibid.*
108 *Ibid.*, para 79.
109 *Prosecutor v Al Mahdi, Confirmation* of Charges Hearing, ICC-01/12-01/15-T-2-Red2-ENG WT 01-03-2016 1/100 SZ PT, 16–21.
110 *Prosecutor v Al Mahdi*, Confirmation of Charges Hearing, ICC-01/12-01/15-T-2-Red2-ENG WT 01-03-2016 1/100 SZ PT, 18.
111 For a discussion of *hisbah*, see Mohamed Elewa Badar and Noelle Higgins, 'Discussion Interrupted: The Destruction and Protection of Cultural Property under International Law and Islamic Law – the Case of *Prosecutor v. Al Mahdi*' (2017) 17(3) *International Criminal Law Review* 486.
112 Mohammad Hashim Kamali, *Freedom of Expression in Islam* (Islamic Texts Society 2010) 28. The principle of 'enjoining what is right and forbidding what is wrong' is reiterated in verse 3:110.
113 Universal Islamic Declaration of Human Rights, adopted by the Islamic Council of Europe on 19 September 1981 http://hrlibrary.umn.edu/instree/islamic_declaration_HR.html accessed 2 October 2017.
114 Imam Muslim, *Sahih Muslim*, translated by Nasiruddin al-Khattab, Vol I (Darussalam Publications 2007), 143–44.
115 Kamarudin bin Ahmad, '*Wilayat Al-Hisbah*; A Means to Achieve Justice and Maintain High Ethical Standards in Societies' (2015) 6 *Mediterranean Journal of Social Sciences* 201, 205.
116 See Mohamed A Mahmoud, Q*uest for Divinity: a Critical Examination of the Thought of Mahmud Muhammad Taha* (Syracuse University Press, 2007), 22.
117 For a discussion of *ziyara*, see Elewa Badar and Higgins (n 111).
118 Hugh Kennedy, *The Early Abbasid Caliphate, A Political History* (Routledge 2016), 48
119 Saïd Amir Arjomand, *Sociology of Shi'ite Islam: Collected Essays* (Brill 2016), 311
120 Y Mirza, 'Abraham as an Iconoclast: Understanding the Destruction of "Images" through Qur'anic Exegesis' (2005) 16 *Islam and Christian–Muslim Relations* 413, 427.
121 *Ibid.*, 416–417.
122 See Elewa Badar and Higgins (n 111), 501–503.
123 *Ibid.*
124 Alison Dundes Renteln (n 43), 278.
125 Article 32(2) of the Rome Statute.
126 Mr Al Mahdi said: 'I am really sorry, I am really remorseful and I regret all the damage that my actions have caused. I regret what I have caused to my family, my community in Timbuktu, what I have caused my home nation, Mali and I'm really remorseful about what I had caused the international community as a whole.' – Transcript of Hearing, 22 August 2016, ICC-01/12-01/15-T-4-Red-ENG, page 8 line 3, to page 9 line 23.

127 UNESCO Submissions, ICC-01/12-01/15-194, para 12.
128 UNESCO Submissions, ICC-01/12-01/15-194, para 12. *Prosecutor v Al Mahdi*, Reparations Order, ICC-01/12-01/15, 17 August 2017, para 116.
129 *Ibid.*
130 *Ibid.*, para 133.
131 *Ibid.*, para 134.
132 *Ibid.*, para 113.
133 Alina Balta and Nadia Banteka, 'The Al-Mahdi Reparations Order at the ICC: A Step towards Justice for Victims of Crimes against Cultural Heritage' (*Opinio Juris*, 6 September 2017).
134 *Prosecutor v Al Mahdi*, First LRV Submissions, ICC-01/12-01/15-190-Red-tENG, paras 110–124.
135 *Prosecutor v Al Mahdi*, Reparations Order, ICC-01/12-01/15, 17 August 2017, para 104.
136 *Ibid.*, para 105.
137 *Prosecutor v Al Mahdi*, Second LRV Submissions, ICC-01/12/01/15-224-Conf-Corr-tENG, para 11.
138 *Prosecutor v Al Mahdi*, Reparations Order, ICC-01/12-01/15, 17 August 2017, para 106.
139 *Ibid.*, para 107.
140 *Prosecutor v Al Mahdi*, Judgment, ICC-01/1201/15-171, para 108.
141 *Prosecutor v Al Mahdi*, Reparations Order, ICC-01/12-01/15, 17 August 2017, para 85.
142 *Plan de Sánchez Massacre v Guatemala*, Judgement (Reparations), 19 November 2004, paras 77, 85–88.
143 *Yakye Axa Indigenous Community v Paraguay*, Judgment (Merits, Reparations and Costs), 17 June 2005, paras 154, 203.
144 *Prosecutor v Al Mahdi*, Reparations Order, ICC-01/12-01/15, 17 August 2017, para 85.
145 *Ibid.*, para 85.
146 *Ibid.*, para 86.
147 a/35000/16, ICC-01/12-01/15-200-Conf-Anx5-Red-tENG, page 2.
148 a/36063/16, ICC-01/12-01/15-200-Conf-Anx56-Red-tENG, page 2.
149 a/35029/16, ICC-01/12-01/15-210-Conf-Anx22-Red-tENG, page 2.
150 *Prosecutor v Al Mahdi*, Reparations Order, ICC-01/12-01/15, 17 August 2017, para 13.
151 *Ibid.*, para 14.

Conclusion

The Rome Statute has been ratified by 123 States,[1] representing various legal traditions and different cultures. Recent statements by a number of States have signalled their desire to withdraw from the Court, and the institution has been plagued with criticism of anti-African bias,[2] and Western imperialism.[3] One of the ways in which the Court could regain some legitimacy in the eyes of its detractors is if it were seen to value all legal traditions equally, and accommodate the cultural concerns of actors who come before it. At the domestic level, one of the ways in which the cultural concerns of minority groups have been addressed within the legal system is through the acceptance of cultural defences. This book has sought, therefore, to analyse whether if, in theory, cultural defences can be raised before the ICC, and whether such defences should be accepted by the Court in practice.

Before attempting to answer these questions, the perceived advantages and disadvantages of cultural defences proffered at the domestic level were considered in Chapter 1. The proposition that courts should allow cultural defences is a very controversial issue in the domestic law realm, with both staunch supporters and strong detractors. While courts in States with multicultural populations have allowed for the cultural context of a defendant's actions to be taken into consideration at various stages of a trial, no State has adopted an official policy accepting such an approach. This has resulted in a very *ad hoc* and uncertain practice in respect of cultural defences domestically. Transplanting the question of cultural defences to the sphere of international law and the ICC is even more controversial, given that the crimes prosecuted by the Court are the most serious crimes of an international nature. However, it can be argued that the nature of the Court, given its jurisdictional reach into numerous States and multifarious cultures, makes a stronger case for the use of defences based on culture, particularly given its reputation as a Western and biased court.[4] Academic commentary on cultural defences in domestic law includes multifarious arguments in favour of, and against, its acceptance. However, one of the most important issues underlined in this discussion is the impact that culture has on an individual's life, and how it shapes their motivations and understandings of the world around them.

Chapter 2 analysed the development of the Court as a cultural actor and its provisions which facilitate cultural sensitivity. This discussion illustrated how other international criminal tribunals have battled with cultural issues in the past, including the International Criminal Tribunal for the former Yugoslavia, the International Criminal Tribunal for Rwanda and the Special Court for Sierra Leone. Some tribunals have been more successful than others in addressing cultural issues and dealing with domestic cultural practices.[5] It is clear that some judges are reluctant, or perhaps, unable, to engage in a legal analysis of domestic customs and cultural practices, with which they are unfamiliar, given their own immersion in Western legal culture. However, this approach delegitimises them in the eyes of the local community in which they are operating. The ICC was heavily influenced by Western legal traditions in its development. This Chapter questioned, therefore, whether its framework left enough room for judges to accommodate cultural considerations and adopt a culturally sensitive approach to legal issues which come before it. It can be seen that a number of the Rome Statute's provisions allow for such an approach to be taken, for example, in relation to the right to an interpreter and the treatment of victims and witnesses. Such provisions leave a lot of discretion up to the judges and it will, therefore, be within their remit to ensure that cultural issues receive due consideration. Another question discussed in this Chapter was whether the use of general principles of law as a source of law under Article 21 of the Rome Statute could act as a 'cultural portal', through which domestic cultural practices may be analysed. However, given the fact that general principles of law can only be referred to if there is no treaty or customary rule, this may not be a common occurrence. One of the main findings of this section of the work is the lack of comparative research undertaken to date on general principles of law, and one of the ways in which cultural considerations could be addressed by institutions such as the ICC is if we, as Drumbl suggests, 'insert comparative law methodologies more deeply into the international jurisprudence'.[6] Bohlander identifies a related issue, finding that when identifying general principles of law at the ICC, there is generally a focus on sources emanating from common and civil law systems, from English language citations, as a result of the (lack of) linguistic abilities of ICC personnel and the books stocked in the institution's library.[7] This is a technical, rather than a substantive, obstacle to ensuring cultural sensitivity and one that the Court should address with urgency.

Chapter 3 discussed the Court's framework concerning defences to analyse if cultural defences could be raised before the Court. Given that the provisions on defences in the ICC Statute are not very detailed, it is concluded that cultural considerations could be encompassed within these provisions, and form an element of a substantive defence. A number of suggestions as to how cultural defences may be formulated were provided in this Chapter. Therefore, in answer to the first question posed in this work, cultural defences can, indeed, be raised before the Court. However, given the paucity of practice on defences before international criminal tribunals, it is uncertain if such approaches would be entertained at the ICC.

Chapter 4 analysed how the Court has dealt with cultural considerations to date. This Chapter illustrated that the Court has addressed cultural issues in depth in some cases, e.g. concerning linguistic diversity, while in others it sidelined them, e.g. consideration of Islamic law principles in the case of *Al Mahdi*. While, to date, no defendant has raised a cultural defence, the approach taken by the Court in respect of cultural considerations, up to now, has been *ad hoc* and uncertain. It seems that a respect for culture and cultural practices does not underpin the Court's approach to legal issues, but rather cultural considerations are at the discretion of the Court.

The second question posed by this book is whether the ICC should accept cultural defences in practice. Given the serious nature of the crimes within the jurisdiction of the Court, it is not suggested that the ICC should allow for a stand-alone cultural defence. To do so would be to undermine the suffering of victims. However, it is argued that the cultural context of a defendant's actions should be allowed to be raised before the Court with respect to the defences set out in Articles 31–33 of the Statute. The raising of cultural factors surrounding a defendant's actions does not mean that the defence should automatically succeed, but rather such an approach would allow for a complete narrative of the crime to be recorded.[8] The Court should then engage fully with a legal analysis of the cultural practice or issue raised, rather than side-step it. Engaging in a discussion of local customs and analysing them against a legal framework is vital for the legitimacy of the Court, and, in this context, Drumbl has urged that we 'integrate non-Western legal traditions into globalized understandings of the adequacy of due process'.[9]

This work has shown that, in addition to allowing the cultural context of a defendant's actions to be raised before the Court, the ICC can also alleviate claims of Western imperialism by utilising to their fullest extent the Rome Statute's provisions that facilitate cultural sensitivity, including in the context of allowing evidence provided by cultural experts on minority legal cultures, and factors to be considered in mitigation of sentence. According to Kelsall: 'Culture matters, and for justice to be done, the international community must adapt to this fact.'[10] The international community, of course, includes the ICC and its personnel. The institution must make a conscious decision to fully recognise the importance of internationally protected cultural rights as well as the undeniable impact of culture on an individual's behaviour in its operation. A culturally sensitive approach should underpin all of the institution's work. Such an approach could manifest in, for example, the stocking of legal sources from a greater range of legal traditions in different languages in the library, the provision of training sessions for judges on minority legal cultures, and full engagement with, and legal analysis of, local cultural practices, including in the context of defences. The ICC framework does allow for a culturally sensitive approach with respect to a number of issues, and it is now incumbent on its legal personnel to embrace this opportunity.

Notes

1 See The States Parties to the Rome Statute, https://asp.icc-cpi.int/en_menus/asp/states%20parties/pages/the%20states%20parties%20to%20the%20rome%20statute.aspx.
2 The perceived anti-African bias has led to a situation whereby members of the African Union have backed a Kenyan proposal to leave the ICC. See Patryk I Labuda, 'The African Union's Collective Withdrawal from the ICC: Does Bad Law make for Good Politics?' (*EJILTalk!*, 15 February, 2017) https://www.ejiltalk.org/the-african-unions-collective-withdrawal-from-the-icc-does-bad-law-make-for-good-politics/ accessed 2 October 2017. Burundi withdrew from the ICC on 27 October 2017.
3 Habeeb Kolade, 'Is the ICC a Western Imperialist Tool against Africa?' (*Swali Africa*, 29 December 2017) http://blog.swaliafrica.com/is-the-icc-a-western-imperialist-tool-against-africa/ accessed 2 October 2017. Burundi withdrew from the ICC on 27 October 2017.
4 See Tim Kelsall, *Culture under Cross-Examination: International Justice and the Special Court for Sierra Leone*, (Cambridge University Press 2009), 8.
5 See Tim Kelsall (n 4); Ida L Bostian, 'Cultural Relativism in International War Crimes Prosecutions: The International Criminal Tribunal for Rwanda' (2005) 12 *International Law Students Association Journal of International and Comparative Law* 1. See also analyses of cultural sensitivity of international criminal tribunals in general by Michael Bohlander, 'Language, Culture, Legal Traditions, and International Criminal Justice' (2014) 12 *Journal of International Criminal Justice* 491; Bing Bing Jia, 'Multiculturalism and the Development of the System of International Criminal Law' in Sienho Yee and Jacques-Yvan Morin (eds), *Multiculturalism and International Law: Essays in Honour of Edward McWhinney* (Martinus Nijhoff 2009); Mark Drumbl, 'Collective Violence and Individual Punishment: The Criminality of Mass Atrocity' (2005) 99 *Northwestern University Law Review* 551; Jessica Almqvist, 'The Impact of Cultural Diversity on International Criminal Proceedings' (2006) 4(4) *Journal of International Criminal Justice* 745; and Fabián O Raimondo, 'For Further Research on the Relationship between Cultural Diversity and International Criminal Law' (2011) 11 *International Criminal Law Review* 299.
6 Mark Drumbl, *Atrocity, Punishment, and International Law* (Cambridge University Press 2007), 207.
7 Michael Bohlander (n 5).

8 Mariniello states that 'it is argued that international criminal tribunals have to provide historiographical reconstruction of the events in a country troubled by civil or international conflicts' – Triestino Mariniello, '"One, No One and One Hundred Thousand'. Reflection on the Multiple Identities of the ICC' in Triestino Maniniello (ed.), *The International Criminal Court in Search of its Purpose and Identity* (Routledge 2015), 1. See also Christine Van den Wyngaert, 'International Criminal Courts as Fact (and Truth) Finders in Post-Conflict Societies: Can Disparities with Ordinary International Courts be Avoided?' in (29 March–1 April 2006) 100 *Proceedings of the Annual Meeting* (American Society of International Law) 63.
9 Mark Drumbl (n 6) 207.
10 Tim Kelsall (n 4), 267.

Bibliography

Akande, Dapo, 'The ICC Assembly of States Parties Prepares to Activate the ICC's Jurisdiction over the Crime of Aggression: But Who Will Be Covered by that Jurisdiction?' (*EJIL:Talk!*, 26 June 2017) www.ejiltalk.org/the-icc-assembly-of-states-parties-prepares-to-activate-the-iccs-jurisdiction-over-the-crime-of-aggression-but-who-will-be-covered-by-that-jurisdiction/ accessed 2 October 2017.

Almqvist, Jessica, 'The Impact of Cultural Diversity on International Criminal Proceedings' (2006) 4(4) *Journal of International Criminal Justice* 745.

Ambos, Kai, *Treatise on International Criminal Law*: Vol I, *Foundations and General Part* (Oxford University Press 2013).

Amirthalingam, Kumaralingam, 'Culture, Crime and Culpability: Perspectives on the Defence of Provocation' in Marie-Claire Foblets and Alison Dundes Renteln (eds), *Multicultural Jurisprudence* (Hart Publishing 2009), 35.

Anthony, Thalia, Bartels, Lorna and Hopkins, Anthony, 'Lessons Lost in Sentencing: Welding Individualised Justice to Indigenous Justice' (2015) 39 *Melbourne University Law Review* 46.

Arjomand, Saïd Amir, *Sociology of Shi'ite Islam: Collected Essays* (Brill 2016).

Ashworth, Andrew, *Principles of Criminal Law* (4th edn, Oxford University Press 2003).

Asimakopoulos, Ariadne, 'Justice and Accountability: Complex Political Perpetrators. Abducted as Children by the LRA in Northern Uganda' (Masters Thesis, Utrecht University 2010).

Azzam, Salem, 'Universal Islamic Declaration of Human Rights' (1998) 2(3) *International Journal of Human Rights* 102.

Bagaric, Mirko and Morss, John, 'International Sentencing Law: In Search of a Justification and Coherent Framework' (2006) 6 *International Criminal Law Review* 191.

Baines, Erin K, 'Complex Political Perpetrators: Reflections on Dominic Ongwen' (2009) 47(2) *Journal of Modern African Studies* 170.

Balta, Alina and Banteka, Nadia, 'The Al-Mahdi Reparations Order at the ICC: A Step towards Justice for Victims of Crimes against Cultural Heritage' (*Opinio Juris*, 6 September 2017) www.opiniojuris.org accessed 11 October 2017.

Bantekas, Ilias and Nash, Susan, *International Criminal Law* (3rd edn, Routledge-Cavendish 2007).

Bantekas, Ilias, 'Legal Anthropology and the Construction of Complex Liabilities' in Charles C Jalloh (ed.) *The Sierra Leone Special Court and Its Legacy: The Impact for Africa and International Criminal Law* (Cambridge University Press 2014), 181.

Barriga, Stefan, 'The Scope of ICC Jurisdiction over the Crime of Aggression: A Different Perspective' (*EJIL: Talk!*, 29 September 2017) www.ejiltalk.org/the-scope-of-icc-jurisdiction-over-the-crime-of-aggression-a-different-perspective accessed 2 October 2017.

Bassiouni, M Cherif, 'Sources of Islamic Law, and the Protection of Human Rights in the Islamic Criminal Justice System' in M Cherif Bassiouni (ed.), *The Islamic Criminal Justice System* (Oceana Publications 1982), 42.

Bassiouni, M Cherif, 'A Functional Approach to General Principles of International Law' (1990) 11 *Michigan Journal of International Law* 768.

Bensouda, Fatou, 'The International Criminal Court and Africa: A Discussion on Legitimacy, Impunity, Selectivity, Fairness and Accountability' (Keynote address, GIMPA Law Conference 2016, Accra, Ghana, 17 March 2016) www.icc-cpi.int/iccdocs/otp/Keynote_Speech_of_the_ProsecutorGIMPA_Law_Conference_on_the_ICC_and_Africa.pdf accessed 2 October 2017.

Bergen-Cico, Dessa K, *War and Drugs: The Role of Military Conflict in the Development of Substance Abuse* (Routledge 2012).

bin Ahmad, Kamarudin, '*Wilayat Al-Hisbah*: A Means to Achieve Justice and Maintain High Ethical Standards in Societies' (2015) 6 *Mediterranean Journal of Social Sciences* 201.

Bohlander, Michael, 'The Influence of Academic Research on the Jurisprudence of the International Tribunal for the Former Yugoslavia – A First Overview' (2003) *The Global Community: Yearbook of International Law and Jurisprudence* 195.

Bohlander, Michael, 'Language, Culture, Legal Traditions, and International Criminal Justice' (2014) 12 *Journal of International Criminal Justice* 491.

Bohlander, Michael and Findlay, Mark, 'The Use of Domestic Sources as a Basis for International Criminal Law Principles' (2002) *The Global Community: Yearbook of International Law and Jurisprudence* 3.

Bostian, Ida L, 'Cultural Relativism in International War Crimes Prosecutions: The International Criminal Tribunal for Rwanda' (2005) 12 *International Law Students Association Journal of International and Comparative Law* 1.

Campbell, Kirsten, 'The Making of Global Legal Culture and International Criminal Law' (2013) 26 *Leiden Journal of International Law* 155.

Canadian Commission for UNESCO, 'A Working Definition of "Culture"', (1977) 4 *Cultures* 78.

Capotorti, Francesco, 'Cours general de droit international public' (1994) 248 *Recueil des cours de l'Académie de droit international de la Haye* 9.

Case Matrix Network, *Commentary on the Rome Statute, Article 103*, www.casematrixnetwork.org/cmn-knowledge-hub/icc-commentary-clicc/commentary-rome-statute/commentary-rome-statute-part-10 accessed 2 October 2017.

Cassese, Antonio, *International Criminal Law* (Oxford University Press 2003)

Cassese, Antonio, 'Achievements and Pitfalls of the ICC Five Years On' in Gabriella Venturini and Stefania Bariatti (eds), *Liber Fausto Pocar* (Giuffré 2009), 147.

Cassese, Antonio and Gaeta, Paola, *Cassese's International Criminal Law* (3rd edn, Oxford University Press 2013).

Caughey, John L, 'The Anthropologist as Expert Witness: A Murder in Maine' in Marie-Claire Foblets and Alison Dundes Renteln (eds), *Multicultural Jurisprudence* (Hart Publishing 2009), 321.

Chiesa, LE, 'Duress, Demanding Heroism and Proportionality' (2008) 41 *Vanderbilt Journal of Transnational Law* 741.

Choi, Carolyn, 'Application of a Cultural Defense in Criminal Proceedings' (1990) 8(1) *Pacific Basin Law Journal* 80.

Christensen, Robert, 'Getting to Peace by Reconciling Notions of Justice: The Importance of Considering Discrepancies between Civil and Common Legal Systems in the Formation of the International Criminal Court' (2001–2002) 6 *UCLA Journal of International Law and Foreign Affairs* 391.

Chroust, Anton-Hermann, 'Aristotle's Conception of Equality (Epieikeia)' (1942) 18(2) *Notre Dame Law Review* 119.

Chuter, David, *War Crimes: Confronting Atrocity in the Modern World* (Lynne Rienner Publishers 2003).

Claes, Erik and Vrielink, Jogchum, 'Cultural Defence and Societal Dynamics' in Marie-Claire Foblets and Alison Dundes Renteln (eds), *Multicultural Jurisprudence* (Hart Publishing 2009), 301.

Coccia, Massimo, 'Reservations to Multilateral Treaties on Human Rights' (1985) 15 *California Western International Law Journal* 1.

Coghlan, Tom and Williams, Sara Elizabeth, 'Suicide Bombers Take Their Courage from Illegal Drugs' *The Times* (28 January 2016) www.thetimes.co.uk/article/suicide-bombers-take-their-courage-from-illegal-drugs-35krdd5wg09 accessed 3 October 2017.

Coleman, DL, 'Individualizing Justice through Multiculturalism: The Liberals' Dilemma' (1996) 96(5) *Columbia Law Review* 1093.

Combs, Nancy A, 'Copping a Plea to Genocide: The Plea Bargaining of International Crimes' (2002) 151(1) *University of Pennsylvania Law Review* 1.

Combs, Nancy A, *Fact-Finding Without Facts: The Uncertain Evidentiary Foundations of International Criminal Convictions* (Cambridge University Press 2010).

Combs, Nancy A, 'Seeking Inconsistency: Advancing Pluralism in International Criminal Sentencing' (2016) 41(1) *Yale Journal of International Law* 1.

Commission on the Responsibility of the Authors of the War and on Enforcement of Penalties, 'Report Presented to the Preliminary Peace Conference, 29 March 1919', reprinted in (1920) 14 *American Journal of International Law* 95.

Cryer, Robert, 'A Long Way from Home: Witnesses before International Criminal Tribunals' (2006) 1 *International Commentary on Evidence* 1.

Cryer, Robert, Friman, Håkan, Robinson, Darryl and Wilmshurst, Elizabeth, *An Introduction to International Criminal Law and Procedure* (3rd edn, Cambridge University Press 2014).

Danilenko, Gennady M, 'The Statute of the International Criminal Court and Third States', (2000) 21 *Michigan Journal of International Law* 445.

Danner, Allison Marston, 'Constructing a Hierarchy of Crimes in International Criminal Law Sentencing' (2001) 87 *Virginia Law Review* 415.

Darcy, Shane, 'The Evolution of the Law of Belligerent Reprisals' (2003) 175 *Military Law Review* 184.

Darcy, Shane, 'Defences to International Crimes' in William Schabas and Nadia Bernaz (eds), *Handbook of International Criminal Law* (Routledge 2011), 231.

David, Eric, *Principes de droit des conflits armés* (2nd edn, Bruylant 1999).

David, R and Brierly, J, *Major Legal Systems in the World Today* (2nd edn, The Free Press 1978).

de Guzman, Margaret, 'Harsh Justice for International Crimes?' (2014) 39 *Yale Journal of International Law* 1.

Derham, Roger and Derham, Nicole, 'From Ad Hoc to Hybrid: The Rules and Regulations Governing Reception of Expert Evidence at the International Criminal Court' (2010) 14 *International Journal of Evidence and Proof* 25.

Donnelly, Jack, 'Cultural Relativism and Universal Human Rights' (1984) 6 *Human Rights Quarterly* 400.

Donovan, James M and Garth, John Stuart, 'Delimiting the Cultural Defense' (2007) 26 *Quinnipiac Law Review* 109.

Drumbl, Mark, 'Collective Violence and Individual Punishment: The Criminality of Mass Atrocity' (2005) 99 *Northwestern University Law Review* 551.

Drumbl, Mark, *Atrocity, Punishment, and International Law* (Cambridge University Press 2007).

Drumbl, Mark, 'The Ongwen Trial at the ICC: Tough Questions on Child Soldiers' (*Open Democracy*, 14 April 2015).

Drumbl, Mark, 'A Former Child Soldier Prosecuted at the International Criminal Court' (*Oxford University Press Blog*, 26 September 2016). https://blog.oup.com/2016/09/child-soldier-prosecuted-icc-law accessed 3 October 2017.

Dundes Renteln, Alison, 'The Child Soldier: The Challenge of Enforcing International Standards' (1999) 21 *Whittier Law Review* 191.

Dundes Renteln, Alison, 'The Use and Abuse of the Cultural Defense' (2005) 20 *Canadian Journal of Law and Society* 47.

Dundes Renteln, Alison, 'The Use and Abuse of the Cultural Defence' in Marie-Claire Foblets and Alison Dundes Renteln (eds), *Multicultural Jurisprudence* (Hart Publishing 2009), 61.

Dundes Renteln, Alison, 'Making Room for Culture in the Court' (2010) 49 *The Judges Journal* 7.

Dundes Renteln, Alison, 'Cultural Defenses in International Criminal Tribunals: A Preliminary Consideration of the Issues' (2011) 18 *Southwestern Journal of International Law* 267.

Dundes Renteln, Alison, 'What Do We Have to Fear from Cultural Defense?' in Will Kymlicka, Claes Lernestedt and Matt Matravers (eds), *Criminal Law and Cultural Diversity* (Oxford University Press 2014), 175.

Dundes Renteln, Alison and Foblets, Marie-Claire, 'Conclusion' in Marie-Claire Foblets and Alison Dundes Renteln (eds), *Multicultural Jurisprudence* (Hart Publishing 2009), 335.

Dundes Renteln, Alison and Valladares, Rene, 'The Importance of Culture for the Justice System' (2009) 92 *Judicature* 193.

du Plessis, Max, Maluwa, Tiyanjana and O'Reilly, Annie, *Africa and the International Criminal Court* (Chatham House Report, International Law 2013/01 2013).

Ehrenreich Brooks, R, 'Law in the Heart of Darkness: Atrocity and Duress' (2003) 43 *Virginia Journal of International Law* 861.

Einar Fife, Rolf, 'Penalties' in Roy S Lee (ed.), *The International Criminal Court: The Making of the Rome Statute* (Kluwer Law 1999), 319.

Elewa Badar, Mohamed, 'Islamic Law (*Shari'a*) and the Jurisdiction of the International Criminal Court' (2011) 24 *Leiden Journal of International Law* 411.

Elewa Badar, Mohamed and Higgins, Noelle, 'General Principles of Law in the Early Jurisprudence of the ICC' in T Mariniello (ed.), *The International Criminal Court in Search of Its Purpose and Identity* (Routledge 2015), 263.

Elewa Badar, Mohamed and Higgins, Noelle, 'Discussion Interrupted: The Destruction and Protection of Cultural Property under International Law and Islamic Law – the Case of *Prosecutor v. Al Mahdi*' (2017) 17(3) *International Criminal Law Review* 486.

Eltringham, Nigel, '"Illuminating the Broader Context": Anthropological and Historical Knowledge at the International Criminal Tribunal for Rwanda' (2013) 19 *Journal of the Royal Anthropological Institute* 338.

Epps, W, 'The Soldier's Obligation to Die when Ordered to Shoot Civilians or Face Death Himself' (2003) 37 *New England Law Review* 987.

Eser, Albin, 'War Crimes Trials' (1995) *Israel Yearbook on Human Rights* 201.

Eser, Albin, 'Defences in War Crimes Trials' in Yoram Dinstein and Mala Tabory (eds), *War Crimes in International Law* (Martinus Nijhoff 1996), 251.

Farrell, Mike, Fletcher, Laurel, Fischer, Barry and Dundes Renteln, Alison, 'War Crimes and other Human Rights Abuses in the Former Yugoslavia' (1995) 16 *Whittier Law Review* 374.

Foblets, M-C, 'Cultural Delicts: The Repercussion of Cultural Conflicts on Delinquent Behaviour. Reflections on the Contribution of Legal Anthropology to a Contemporary Debate' (1998) 6 *European Journal of Crime, Criminal Law and Criminal Justice* 187.

Freeman Jalet, Frances T, 'The Quest for the General Principles of Law Recognized by Civilized Nations: A Study' (1963) 10 *University of California Los Angeles Law Review* 1041.

Frulli, Micaela, 'The Criminalization of Offences against Cultural Heritage in Times of Armed Conflict: The Quest for Consistency' (2011) 22(1) *European Journal of International Law* 203.

Glendon, Mary Ann, *Comparative Legal Traditions in a Nutshell* (West Publishing Company 1982).

Grant, Nadia, *Duress as a Defence for Former Child Soldiers? Dominic Ongwen and the International Criminal Court* (International Crimes Database Brief 21, December 2016).

Green Martínez, Sebastián A, 'Destruction of Cultural Heritage in Northern Mali: A Crime Against Humanity?' (2015) 13(5) *Journal of International Criminal Justice* 1073.

Greenawalt, Alexander KA, 'The Pluralism of International Criminal Law' (2011) 86 *Indiana Law Journal* 1063.

Grossman, Nienke, 'Rehabilitation or Revenge: Prosecuting Child Soldiers for Human Rights Violations' (2007) 38 *Georgetown Journal of International Law* 323.

Hafner, Gerhard and Binder, Christina, 'The Interpretation of Article 21(3) ICC Statute Opinion Reviewed' (2004) 9 *Austrian Review of International and European Law* 163.

Hampson, Françoise, 'Military Necessity' in Roy Gitman and David Rieff (eds), *Crimes of War: What the Public Should know* (WW Norton & Company 1999), 251.

Heller, Kevin Jon, 'Beyond the Reasonable Man? A Sympathetic but Critical Assessment of the Use of Subjective Standards of Reasonableness in Self-Defense and Provocation Cases' (1998) 26 *American Journal of Criminal Law* 1.

Henckaerts, Jean-Marie and Doswald-Beck, Louise, *Customary Humanitarian Law. Volume I: Rules* (ICRC/Cambridge University Press 2005).

Higgins, Noelle and Elewa Badar, Mohamed, 'The Destruction of Cultural Property in Timbuktu: Challenging the ICC War Crime Paradigm', forthcoming *Europa Ethnica* (2017).

Human Rights Watch, *Coercion and Intimidation of Child Soldiers to Participate in Violence* (Human Rights Watch Report, 16 April 2008) www.hrw.org/news/2008/04/16/coercion-and-intimidation-child-soldiers-participate-violence accessed 3 October 2017.

Humphrey, J, 'The International Bill of Rights and Implementation: Scope and Implementation' (1976) 17 *William and Mary Law Review* 527.

Hussa, Jacko, 'Classification of Legal Families Today: Is It Time for Memorial Hymn?' (2004) 56(1) *Revue Internationale de Droit Comparé* 11.

Jalet, Frances T Freeman, 'The Quest for the General Principles of Law Recognized by Civilized Nations: A Study' (1963) 10 *UCLA Law Review* 1041.

Jia, Bing Bing, 'Multiculturalism and the Development of the System of International Criminal Law' in Sienho Yee and Jacques-Yvan Morin (eds), *Multiculturalism and International Law: Essays in Honour of Edward McWhinney* (Martinus Nijhoff 2009).

Joyce, Marcus, 'Duress: From Nuremberg to the International Criminal Court; Finding the Balance between Justification and Excuse' (2015) 28(3) *Leiden Journal of International Law* 623.

Justice and Reconciliation Project, *Complicating Victims and Perpetrators in Uganda: On Dominic Ongwen* (Field Note 7, July 2008).

Kamali, Mohammad Hashim, *Freedom of Expression in Islam* (Islamic Texts Society 2010).

Kaplan, Eben, *Child Soldiers around the World* (Council on Foreign Relations, 2 December 2005)

Karton, Joshua, 'Lost in Translation: International Criminal Tribunals and the Legal Implications of Interpreted Testimony' (2008) 41(1) *Vanderbildt Journal of Transnational Law* 1.

Kelsall, Tim, *Culture under Cross-Examination: International Justice and the Special Court for Sierra Leone* (Cambridge University Press 2009).

Kennedy, Hugh, *The Early Abbasid Caliphate: A Political History* (Routledge 2016).

Kirsch, P and Oosterveld, V, 'Negotiating an Institution for the Twenty-First Century: Multilateral Diplomacy and the International Criminal Court' (2001) 46 *McGill Law Journal* 1141.

Knoops, Geert-Jan Alexander, *Defences in Contemporary International Criminal Law* (2nd edn, Martinus Nijhoff 2008).

Kolade, Habeeb, 'Is the ICC a Western Imperialist Tool against Africa?' (*Swali Africa*, 29 December 2017) http://blog.swaliafrica.com/is-the-icc-a-western-imperialist-tool-against-africa/ accessed 2 October 2017.

Koomen, Jonneke, 'Language Work at International Criminal Courts' (2014) 16(4) *International Feminist Journal of Politics* 581.

Koskenniemi, Martti, *From Apology to Utopia* (Cambridge University Press 1989).

Krasnostein, Sarah, 'Too Much Individualisation, Not Enough Justice' (2014) 39(1) *Alternative Law Journal* 12.

Krebs, Beatrice, 'Justification and Excuse in Article 31(1) of the Rome Statute' (2010) 2(3) *Cambridge Journal of International and Comparative Law* 382.

Krug, Peter, 'The Emerging Mental Incapacity Defense in International Criminal Law: Some Initial Questions of Implementation' (2000) 94(2) *American Journal of International Law* 317.

Kurth, Michael E, 'The *Lubanga* Case of the International Criminal Court: A Critical Analysis of the Trial Chamber's Findings on Issues of Active Use, Age, and Gravity' (2013) 5(2) *Goettingen Journal of International Law* 431.

Kusters, Joke, 'Criminalising Romani Culture through Law' in Marie-Claire Foblets and Alison Dundes Renteln (eds), *Multicultural Jurisprudence* (Hart Publishing 2009), 199.

Kymlicka, Will, Lernestedt, Claes and Matravers, Matt, 'Introduction: Criminal Law and Cultural Diversity' in Will Kymlicka, Claes Lernestedt and Matt Matravers (eds), *Criminal Law and Cultural Diversity* (Oxford University Press 2014), 1.

Labuda, Patryk I, 'The African Union's Collective Withdrawal from the ICC: Does Bad Law Make for Good Politics?' (*EJILTalk!*, 15 February, 2017) www.ejiltalk.org/the-african-unions-collective-withdrawal-from-the-icc-does-bad-law-make-for-good-politics/ accessed 2 October 2017.

Lee, Roy S (ed.), *The International Criminal Court: The Making of the Rome Statute* (Kluwer Law 1999).

Lernestedt, Claes, 'Criminal Law and "Culture"' in Will Kymlicka, Claes Lernestedt and Matt Matravers (eds), *Criminal Law and Cultural Diversity* (Oxford University Press 2014), 15.

Lew, J and Shore, L, 'International Commercial Arbitration: Harmonizing Cultural Differences' (1999) 54 *Dispute Resolution Journal* 33.

LRA Crisis Tracker, *Update: The State of the LRA in 2015* (September 2015).

Magliveras, Konstantinos D and Naldi, Gino J, 'The International Criminal Courts Involvement with Africa: Evaluation of a Fractious Relationship' (2013) 82(3) *Nordic Journal of International Law* 417.

Mahmoud, Mohamed A, *Quest For Divinity: A Critical Examination of the Thought of Mahmud Muhammad Taha* (Syracuse University Press 2007).

Mariniello, Triestino, '"One, No One and One Hundred Thousand'. Reflection on the Multiple Identities of the ICC' in Triestino Maniniello (ed.), *The International Criminal Court in Search of its Purpose and Identity* (Routledge 2015), 1.

Matravers, Matt, 'Responsibility, Morality, and Culture' in Will Kymlicka, Claes Lernestedt and Matt Matravers (eds), *Criminal Law and Cultural Diversity* (Oxford University Press 2014), 89.

McAuliffe de Guzman, Margaret, 'Article 21: Applicable Law' in Otto Triffterer (ed.) *Commentary on the Rome Statute of the International Criminal Court* (Nomos Verlagsgesellschaft 1999), 435.

Mirza, Y, 'Abraham as an Iconoclast: Understanding the Destruction of "Images" through Qur'anic Exegesis' (2005) 16 *Islam and Christian–Muslim Relations* 413.

Muslim, Imam, *Sahih Muslim*, translated by Nasiruddin al-Khattab, Vol I (Darussalam Publications 2007), 143–44.

Mutaizibwa, Emma, *LRA Under Pressure to Back Peace Plan* (Institute for War and Peace Reporting, 20 December 2007).

Mutua, Makau W, 'What is TWAIL?' (2002) American Society of International Law, Proceedings of the 94th Annual Meeting 31.

Nassar, Ahmad E, 'The International Criminal Court and the Applicability of International Jurisdiction under Islamic Law' (2003) 4(2) *Chicago Journal of International Law* 587.

Nolen, Stephanie and Baines, Eric, 'The Making of a Monster' *The Globe and Mail* (25 October 2008) https://beta.theglobeandmail.com/news/world/the-making-of-a-monster/article20389116/?ref=http://www.theglobeandmail.com& accessed 2 October 2017.

Nuotio, Kimmo, 'Between Denial and Recognition: Criminal Law and Cultural Diversity' in Will Kymlicka, Claes Lernestedt and Matt Matravers (eds), *Criminal Law and Cultural Diversity* (Oxford University Press 2014), 85.

Ocampo, Luis Moreno, 'The Role of International Judicial Bodies in Administering the Rule of Law' (Remarks made at the Qatar Law Forum, 30 May 2009).

Olayemi, Abdul Azeez Maruf, Abdul Majeed Hamzah Alabi and Ahmad Hidayah Buang, 'Islamic Human Rights Law: A Critical Evaluation of UIDHR & CDHRI in Context of UDHR' (2015) 1(3) *Journal of Islam, Law and Judiciary* 27.

Parekh, Bhikhu, 'Cultural Defense and the Criminal Law' in Will Kymlicka, Claes Lernestedt and Matt Matravers (eds), *Criminal Law and Cultural Diversity* (Oxford University Press 2014), 104.

Pellet, Alain, 'Applicable Law' in Antonio Cassese, Paola Gaeta, and John RWD Jones (eds) *The Rome Statute of the International Criminal Court: A Commentary*, Vol II (Oxford University Press 2002), 1051.

Perrin, Benjamin, 'An Emerging International Criminal Law Tradition: Gaps in Applicable Law and Transnational Common Law' (Institute of Comparative Law, McGill Faculty of Law, Montreal, 2007).

Picker, Colin B, 'International Law's Mixed Heritage: A Common/Civil Law Jurisdiction' (2008) 41 *Vanderbildt Journal of Transnational Law* 1083.

Powell, Emilia Justyna and Mitchell, Sara, 'The International Court of Justice and the World's Three Legal Systems' (2007) 69(2) *The Journal of Politics* 397.

Powell, Emilia Justyna and Mitchell, Sara, 'The Creation and Expansion of the International Criminal Court: A Legal Explanation' (Midwest Political Science Association Conference, Chicago, Illinois, 3–6 April 2008) http://ir.uiowa.edu/polisci_pubs/3/ accessed 2 October 2017

Provost, René, 'Magic and Modernity in Tintin au Congo (1930) and the Sierra Leone Special Court' (2012) 16 *Law Text Culture* 183.

Raimondo, Fabián O, *General Principles of Law in the Decisions of International Criminal Courts and Tribunals* (Martinus Nijhoff 2008).

Raimondo, Fabián O, 'For Further Research on the Relationship between Cultural Diversity and International Criminal Law' (2011) 11 *International Criminal Law Review* 299.

Rauxloh, Regina, 'Case Comment: Decision on the Defence Request Concerning Languages, Prosecutor v. Katanga' in André Klip and Steven Freeland (eds), *Annotated Leading Cases of International Criminal Tribunals* (Intersentia 2014), 664.

Rhodes, John, 'Up in Smoke: The Religious Freedom Restoration Act and Federal Marijuana Prosecutions' (2015) 38 *Oklahoma City University Law Review* 319.

Roach, Steven, 'Arab States and the Role of Islam in the International Criminal Court' (2005) 53 *Political Studies* 143.

Rowe, Peter, 'Duress as a Defence to War Crimes after Erdemović: A Laboratory for a Permanent Court?' (1998) 1 *Yearbook of International Humanitarian Law* 210.

Safferling, Christoph, *International Criminal Procedure* (Oxford University Press 2012).

Sagartz, A, 'Resolution of International Commercial Disputes: Surmounting Barriers of Culture without Going to Court' (1997–1998) 13 *Ohio State Journal of Dispute Resolution* 675.

Sahar, A and Sluiter, G, *International Criminal Law* (Oxford University Press 2008).

Saland, Per, 'International Criminal Law Principles' in Roy SK Lee (ed.), *The International Criminal Court: The Making of the Rome Statute* (Martinus Nijhoff 1999), 189.

Sams, Julia P, 'The Availability of the "Cultural Defense" as an Excuse for Criminal Behavior' (1986) 16 *Georgia Journal of International and Comparative Law* 335.

Sander, Barrie, 'The Expressive Limits of International Criminal Justice: Victim Trauma and Local Culture in the Iron Cage of the Law' (2016) iCourts Working Paper Series, No 38 2016 https://papers.ssrn.com/sol3/papers.cfm?abstract_id=2711236 accessed 2 October 2017.

Sanders, Clinton R, 'Doper's Wonderland: Functional Drug Use by Military Personnel in Vietnam' (1973) 3(1) *Journal of Drug Issues* 65.

Schabas, William, 'Sentencing by International Tribunals: A Human Rights Approach' (1997) 7 *Duke Journal of Comparative and International Law* 461.

Schabas, William, *The UN International Criminal Tribunals* (Cambridge University Press 2006).

Schabas, William, *An Introduction to the International Criminal Court* (4th edn, Cambridge University Press 2011).

Schabas, William, 'Al Mahdi Has Been Convicted of a Crime He Did Not Commit' (2017) 49 *Case Western Reserve Journal of International Law* 75.

Schacht, J, *An Introduction to Islamic Law* (Clarendon Press 2002).

Scharf, Michael P, 'Results of the Rome Conference for an International Criminal Court' (August 1998) 3 (10) *The American Society of International Law Insights*. www.asil.org/insights/volume/3/issue/10/results-rome-conference-international-criminal-court accessed 7 November 2017.

Schauer, E and Elbert, T, 'The Psychological Impact of Child Soldiering' in E Martz (ed.), *Trauma Rehabilitation After War and Conflict* (Springer 2010), 311.

Schlesinger, Rudolf B, 'Research on the General Principles of Law Recognized by Civilized Nations' (1957) 51 *American Journal of International Law* 734.

Schomburg, W and Peterson, I, 'Genuine Consent to Sexual Violence under International Criminal Law' (2007) 101(1) *American Journal of International Law* 121.

Schweda, Nicholson Nancy, 'Interpreting at the International Criminal Court: Linguistic Issues and Challenges' (EULITA Conference Antwerp November 2009) http://eulita.eu/sites/default/files/Interpreting%20at%20the%20ICC.pdf accessed 2 October 2017.

Shaw, Malcolm N, *International Law* (6th edn, Cambridge University Press 2008).

Sheppard, A, 'Child Soldiers: Is the Optional Protocol Evidence of an Emerging "Straight 18" Consensus?' (2000) 8(1) *International Journal of Children's Rights* 37.

Silva, Natalia, 'Mental Insanity at the International Criminal Court: Proposal for a New Regulation' in Mark D White (ed.), *The Insanity Defense: Multidisciplinary Views on its History, Tends and Controversies* (Praeger 2017), 307.

Sloane, Robert D, 'Sentencing for the Crime of Crimes: The Evolving "Common Law" of Sentencing of the International Criminal Tribunal for Rwanda' (2007) 5 *Journal of International Criminal Justice* 713.

Snelders, Stephen and Pieters, Toine, 'Speed in the Third Reich: Metamphetamine (Pervitin) Use and a Drug History From Below' (2011) 24(1) *Social History of Medicine* 686.

Stallard, A, 'Joining the Culture Club: Examining Cultural Context when Implementing International Dispute Resolution' (2002) 17 *Ohio State Journal of Dispute Resolution* 463.

Stamatopoulou, Elsa, *The Right to Culture in International Law* (Brill 2007).

Swigart, Leigh, 'Linguistic and Cultural Diversity in International Criminal Justice: Toward Bridging the Divide' (2016) 48 *University of the Pacific Law Review* 197.

Traer, Robert, 'Religious Communities in the Struggle for Human Rights', *Christian Century*, (28 September 1988) 836.

Truffin, Barbara and Arjona, César, 'The Cultural Defence in Spain' in Marie-Claire Foblets and Alison Dundes Renteln (eds), *Multicultural Jurisprudence* (Hart Publishing 2009), 85.

Truth and Reconciliation Commission of Liberia, *Final Report of the Truth and Reconciliation Commission of Liberia* (Volume I: Findings and Recommendations, 2009).

UNESCO instruments on cultural property, http://portal.unesco.org/en/ev.php-URL_ID=13649&URL_DO=DO_TOPIC&URL_SECTION=-471.html accessed 2 October 2017.

UNESCO, *Protecting Cultural Heritage: An Imperative for Humanity* (Report for the United Nations, 22 September 2016) www.unesco.se/wp-content/uploads/2016/09/2016-Protecting-cultural-heritage.-An-imperative....pdf accessed 2 October 2017.

United Nations Security Council. *Report of the Secretary-General on the Activities of United Nations Regional Office for Central Africa and on the Lord's Resistance Army-affected Areas* (S/2013/297, May 2013).

Van Broeck, Jeroen, 'Cultural Defence and Culturally Motivated Crimes (Cultural Offences) (2001) 9(1) *European Journal of Crime, Criminal Law and Criminal Justice* 1.

van den Herik, Larissa, 'Economic, Social and Cultural Rights: International Criminal Law's Blind Spot?' in E Riedel, C Golay, C Mahon and G Giacca (eds), *Economic, Social and Cultural Rights: Contemporary Issues and Challenges* (Oxford University Press 2013), 343.

Van den Wyngaert, Christine, 'International Criminal Courts as Fact (and Truth) Finders in Post-Conflict Societies: Can Disparities with Ordinary International Courts be Avoided?' in (29 March–1 April 2006) 100 *Proceedings of the Annual Meeting* (American Society of International Law) 63.

van Sliedregt, Elies and Vasiliev, Sergey, *Pluralism in International Criminal Law* (Oxford University Press 2014).

Vasiliev, Sergey, 'Proofing the Ban on "Witness Proofing": Did the ICC Get it Right?' (2009) 20(2) *Criminal Law Forum* 193.

Voigt, Christina, 'The Role of General Principles in International Law and their Relationship to Treaty Law' (2008) 31(2) *Retfaerd Årgang* 5.

Wald, Patricia M, 'The International Criminal Tribunal for the Former Yugoslavia Comes of Age: Some Observations on Day-to-Day Dilemmas of an International Court' (2001) 5 *Washington University Journal of Law and Policy* 87.

Waldman, E, 'Identifying the Role of Social Norms in Mediation: A Multiple Model Approach' (1997) 48 *Hastings Law Journal* 703.

War Child, *The Lord's Resistance Army Profile* www.warchild.org.uk/issues/the-lords-resostance-army accessed 2 October 2017.

Wiener, Noam, 'Excuses, Justifications, and Duress at the International Criminal Tribunals' (2014) 26(2) *Pace International Law Review* 88.

Wilson, Richard Ashby, 'Expert Evidence on Trial: Social Researchers in the International Criminal Courtroom' (2016) 43(4) *American Ethnologist* 730.

Woodman, Gordon R, 'The Culture Defence in English Common Law: the Potential for Development' in Marie-Claire Foblets and Alison Dundes Renteln (eds), *Multicultural Jurisprudence* (Hart Publishing 2009), 7.

York, Geoffrey, 'ICC trial on destruction of Timbuktu shrines debates meaning of Islam' *The Globe and Mail* (1 March 2016) www.theglobeandmail.com/news/world/icc-trial-on-destruction-of-timbuktu-shrines-debates-meaning-of-islam/article28989152/ accessed 2 October 2017.

Young, Rebecca, '"Internationally Recognized Human Rights" before the International Criminal Court' (2011) 60(1) *International and Comparative Law Quarterly* 189.

Index

Page numbers followed by 'n' refer to chapter notes, with the number following the 'n' indicating the note number.

122   *Index*

For Product Safety Concerns and Information please contact our EU
representative GPSR@taylorandfrancis.com
Taylor & Francis Verlag GmbH, Kaufingerstraße 24, 80331 München, Germany

www.ingramcontent.com/pod-product-compliance
Ingram Content Group UK Ltd.
Pitfield, Milton Keynes, MK11 3LW, UK
UKHW021422080625
459435UK00011B/124